# 12

# Steps to a Better Memory

## Carol A. Turkington

MACMILLAN • USA

*For my sister Barbara*

Macmillan General Reference
A Simon & Schuster Macmillan Company
1633 Broadway
New York, NY 10019-6785

An Arco Book

Library of Congress Cataloging-in-Publication Data
Turkington, Carol.
12 steps to a better memory / Carol A. Turkington
p. cm.
ISBN 0-02-860579-9
1. Mnemonics. 2. Memory. I. Title
BF385.T87 1996
153.1'4—dc20 95-37513
CIP

Manufactured in the United States of America
10 9 8 7 6 5 4 3 2 1

# Contents

**Introduction**

## Step 1. Understand How Memory Works

Where Is Memory?
How Memories Begin
How Memories Are Recorded
How Memories Are Retrieved
The Three Stages of Memory Formation
Memory Lapses
IQ and Memory
Sleep Learning
Memory Improvement Techniques

## Step 2. Recognize the Keys to a Better Memory

Key 1. Pay Attention
Key 2. Associate
Key 3. Visualize

# Step 3. Improve Your Everyday Memory

Everyday Forgetting
Remembering Places
Remembering Everyday Information
Keeping Track of Dates and Appointments
Conquering Absentmindedness
Remembering Quantities
Recalling Where You Put Things
Keeping to Schedules
Thinking Up Your Own Strategies

# Step 4. Learn the Method of Loci

Following in the Footsteps of Memory
Expanding Your Loci System

# Step 5. Follow the Link Method

The Limitations of Links
Practicing Linking
The Story System
How Effective Are the Link and Story Systems?

# Step 6. Master the Peg System

What Is the Peg System?
The Rhyming-Peg Method
Alphabet Pegs
Other Peg Systems
Phonetic Pegs

# Step 7. Remember Names

What's Your Name Again?
Verbal Techniques for Remembering Names
Visual Techniques for Remembering Names

# Step 8. Remember Speeches and Foreign Languages

Mnemonic Techniques for Speakers
Foreign Language Techniques

# Step 9. Remember Numbers

Chunking
Simple Visualization
Numerical Relationships
Secret-Code Method
Phonetic Peg System
Picture Code
Aerobic Exercise
Twelve-Digit Code for Dates

# Step 10. Improve Your Study Methods

Techniques for Recording Information
The PQRST Method
Make the Most of Your Study Time
Use Peg Systems in Your Studies
Try Link Systems to Learn
Experiment with the Method of Loci

## Step 11. Maintain Memory with Age

How Memory Ages
How to Improve Your Memory

## Step 12. Improve Your Memory Through Your Lifestyle

Stress and Memory
When Your Mind Goes Blank
Diet and Memory
Sleep and Memory
Medication and Memory
Alcohol and Memory
Smoking and Memory
Caffeine and Memory

## Glossary

## Bibliography

# Introduction

People often talk about their memory as if it were a *thing,* like a bad heart or a good head of hair, but in fact memory doesn't exist in the way an object exists. Rather, memory refers to the *process* of remembering.

Contrary to popular belief, our memories aren't plucked fully formed out of little file cabinets stored in our heads; they represent an incredibly complex constructive power we each possess.

While most people speak of having a "bad memory" or a "good memory," most people are good at remembering some things and not so good at remembering others. When a person has trouble remembering something, it's generally not the fault of the entire memory system—just an inefficient component in that system.

For example, if a person wants to remember where he places his keys, he must first become aware of where he puts them when he walks in the door. He *registers* what he does by paying attention to the action of putting his keys down on the hall table. This information is then retained, ready to be retrieved at a later date. If the memory system is working properly, he can remember exactly where he left his keys. If he has forgotten where he put his keys, one of several things could have happened:

- He may not have registered clearly to start with.
- He may not have retained what he registered.
- He may not be able to retrieve the memory accurately.

There are many factors that go into how well a memory is formed, including how familiar the information is and how much attention has been paid. Good health also plays a major part in how well a person remembers.

But while scientists don't fully understand *how* a person remembers or what occurs during recall, they've learned that it is possible to improve the memory process. Practicing memorization can help improve memory—but what a person does during that practice is more important than how much time is spent. One study found that three hours of general memory practice did not improve long-term memory, but three hours of practicing using certain techniques did.

By learning a few simple techniques, it's possible to remember a great deal of information that you once routinely forgot. And while most people assume that memory loss is an inescapable reality among the aging, this is simply not true.

*12 Steps to a Better Memory* is a step-by-step discussion of detailed techniques for improving memory for names, lists, speeches, foreign languages, faces, addresses, and numbers. In addition, this book includes a chapter discussing memory and aging. Since memory loss is not an inevitable side effect of age, you will learn techniques based on neuropsychological research that can help prevent memory loss—and even reverse the decline of memory in otherwise healthy people, if it has already begun.

# S T E P

# Understand How Memory Works

Whether it's the date of your spouse's birthday or where you left the keys to your car, nothing is more frustrating than not being able to remember something. Forgetting may also have more serious consequences, as when you can't remember information for a test or forget an important business appointment.

Before getting into a discussion of how to improve your memory by learning new behaviors and memory strategies, it's a good idea to have an idea of how we form and recall memories in the first place.

Memory is really not so much a retrieval as it is an active construction. If you say that you know something, you're really speaking metaphorically—you're assuming that you can construct the answer. Contrary to beliefs in past centuries, memories do not exist as fully formed bits of flotsam in your brain.

# Where Is Memory?

At present, the seat of memory cannot be found in any one place in the brain. Instead, scientists believe memory actually functions on a much more basic level—the level of synapses scattered in weblike patterns throughout the brain. In fact, scientists don't really make any distinction between how you remember and how you think. No one completely understands either process. The quest to discover how the brain organizes memories and where those memories are acquired and stored is a continuing challenge for brain researchers.

In order to study memory, traditional researchers have used drugs or surgery on animals to affect parts of the brain, and then applied behavioral tests to measure those effects. These experiments have shown that memory is a biological phenomenon with its roots firmly in the senses—sight, sound, smell, touch, kinesthetic, and so on.

# How Memories Begin

The latest research suggests that memories begin with perception. If your earliest memory is of nestling in the arms of your mother, your visual system identified the attributes of objects in space: "This shape is Mother's face, this shape is a sweater, this is its color, this is its smell, this is how it feels."

Each of these separate sensations then travels to the part of the brain that integrates the perceptions as they occur into a single, memorable moment, binding them into the experience of being held by Mother. The brain then consolidates information for storage as permanent memory. Thus, memory and perception are intertwined in a subtle and unbreakable bond that unites all of our experiences.

However, it is possible to speak of visual memory and verbal memory as two separate things. About 60 percent of Americans have a visual memory, easily visualizing places, faces, or the pages of a newspaper. The rest seem better able to remember sounds or words, and the associations they think of are often rhymes or puns.

# How Memories Are Recorded

Understanding the link between memory and perception provides only part of the picture. While memory does indeed begin with perception, many researchers believe that memories are recorded by electricity. Nerve cells connect with other brain cells at junctions called synapses; the cells fire electrical signals to each other across these junctions, which triggers the release of brain chemicals. The human brain contains about 10 billion of these nerve cells joined by about 60 trillion synapses.

The wispy tips of the brain cells that receive these electrical impulses—the dendrites—seem to play an important role in memory. It is suspected that when an electrical impulse reaches a brain cell (perhaps carrying the information of a seven-digit phone number), the impulse compresses the dendrite. When the dendrite springs back into its usual shape, the electrical pulse disappears, along with the phone number. This, then, could be the mechanism of short-term memory.

Most scientists believe that memory occurs as a result of functional changes in synapses or dendrites caused by the effects of external stimuli prompted by training or education. And while memory can be found throughout the brain, many scientists also believe that various specialized types of information are contained within specific areas of the brain. It might be that the consolidation of this information into a thought or image requires multiple nerve-cell firings in different parts of the brain. Researchers have found that nerve cells in separate parts of the brain fire rhythmically and together when responding to visual stimuli that appear to come from the same object.

# How Memories Are Retrieved

It does seem to be true that anything that influences behavior leaves a trace somewhere in the nervous system. Theoretically, as long as these memory traces last, they can be restimulated, and the event or experience that established them will be remembered. The brain appears to retrieve memories by using a single moment or sensation to trigger recall of others: the smell of your mother's perfume or the feel of a soft sweater brings with it the memory of *mother*. Each time the memory is called up, the brain strengthens the connections between the various elements of each perception. It is only after years of such recall that a memory is laid down permanently in storage, where it can be called up without the aid of a particular area of the brain. The study of memory, then, tries to find out how to identify the conditions for the persistence of memory traces and how to restimulate them.

While people often think of memory as a single phenomenon, in fact there are two distinct mechanisms, corresponding to different mental processes—voluntary and involuntary memory. The smell of your mother's perfume may trigger an involuntary memory if the sensation comes by surprise, or your memory of her may appear as a voluntary memory if you choose to search for it.

# The Three Stages of Memory Formation

While most people think of long-term memory when they say "memory," in fact information must first be perceived and then pass through short-term memory before it can be stored in long-term memory.

## Registration

Formation of a memory begins with registering the information during perception. The data is then filed in a short-term memory system that seems to be quite limited in the amount of material that it can store at any one time. Unless the information is constantly repeated, material in short-term memory is lost within minutes and is replaced by other material. (Think of how long you can retain a phone number between the time you look it up in the phone book and the time you dial it. Most people can retain it only if they keep repeating it aloud as they dial.)

## Retention

Important material is not lost, but is transferred to long-term memory and retained. The process of storage involves making associations between words, meanings, visual imagery, or other experiences such as smells or sounds. People tend to store material on subjects they already know something about, because this information has more meaning for them. This is why a person with a normal memory may be able to remember one subject in great depth. In addition, people remember words that are related to something they already know, because there is already a "file" in their memory related to that information.

## Recall

The final stage of memory is recall, in which information stored on the unconscious level is brought up into the conscious mind. How reliable this material is, researchers believe, depends on how well it was originally encoded.

# Memory Lapses

While most people speak of having a "bad memory" or a "good memory," in fact most people are good at remembering some things and not so good at remembering others. If you have memory problems, this probably means that some part of the process has developed a glitch. It doesn't necessarily mean that your entire memory system is starting to self-destruct.

Can't remember where you parked your car? Try paying attention to your surroundings; notice unusual landmarks as you remove the key, open the door, and get out of the car. This will help you find your car later. If you forget, one of several things might have happened. You may not have been paying close attention to start with, you may not have retained what you registered, or you may not be able to retrieve the memory accurately.

Research suggests that older people can have trouble with all three of these stages, but they have particular problems with registering and retrieving information. But if people of any age want to improve their memory, they must work on improving all three stages of the memory process.

Many factors go into how well a memory is formed, including how familiar the information is and how much attention has been paid to it. Good health also plays a major part in how well a person performs intentional memory tasks. When mental and physical conditions aren't the best, the entire memory system functions at a slower pace, diminishing attention (the key to good memory performance) and weakening long-term memory. Ideas and images are not likely to be registered as strongly, and memory traces become fainter, making them harder to retrieve or file into long-term memory. In fact, patients who get sick often have significantly more memory problems than those who enjoy good health, according to a survey of 1,000 subjects by the National Center of Health Statistics.

# IQ and Memory

People with high IQs generally have good memories, although some people have exceptionally good memories that seem to be unrelated to intellectual functioning. There are even some people with serious mental disabilities who have profoundly intense memories for specific types of information—the so-called autistic savants.

Nearly 10 percent of children diagnosed with autism may be classified as savants. No matter what their particular talent, all savants share a prodigious memory; their skills may appear in a range of areas, including calendar calculating, music, rapid arithmetic, art, or mechanical ability. One of the more common patterns that can be found among savants is a triad of mental retardation, blindness, and musical ability.

# Sleep Learning

While it is popularly believed that a person can learn and remember better while sleeping, in fact research has shown that learning does not take place while you are sound asleep. If you play an educational tape while you're asleep and you learn some of the material, you have actually remembered what you heard during a waking period.

However, there is some evidence suggesting that you can learn while you are very drowsy, or even in a very light sleep. The material must be presented at just the right time; if you aren't sleepy enough, the material will wake you up, and if you're too deeply asleep, the material won't make an impression at all. In addition, complex material involving reasoning or understanding can't be learned while in this drowsy state.

What can be learned during this period are nonsense syllables, Morse code, facts, dates, foreign languages, and the like. But this type of drowsy learning is not enough on its own; it is effective only if used along with daytime learning.

On the other hand, falling asleep immediately after learning something does help you retain the information better than if you stayed up and participated in another activity. And a good night's sleep will help make you alert for memory tasks the next day. This doesn't mean that taking sleeping pills will help you remember, however. The lingering effects of these drugs will make you less able to register new memories the next day, and you'll be less responsive to stimulation that can help you remember already-learned information.

# Memory Improvement Techniques

Fortunately for all of us who have trouble learning while sleeping, there are a number of techniques for improving memory that can be learned while you're awake, and they will be explored in depth in this book. Because remembering is a learned skill, it can be developed just like any other type of skill. Learning anything takes time, patience, practice, and experience, and the same is true for memory improvement techniques. It's not a matter of learning one or two "tricks" and having a good memory for life. In fact, studies

Consolidation Periods followed by
spaced review

Falling asleep immediately after learning something can help you retain that information

show that adults who remain mentally active by maintaining their reading and study habits are able to remember what they read better than those who aren't mentally active.

While you may have given up on your memory in despair, it's important to understand that actual differences in memory ability are not nearly as important as differences in learned memory skills. How good your memory really is depends on how well you've learned memory techniques, not any function of innate memory ability. Therefore, if you learn more memory strategies, you'll automatically improve your memory.

S T E P

# Recognize the Keys to a Better Memory

One of the best-known examples of a person with a remarkable memory was a Russian newspaper reporter named Shereshevskii, who was a patient of the great Russian neuropsychologist Alexandr Luria. In 1968, Luria wrote about Shereshevskii (whom he called simply "S.") in *The Mind of a Mnemonist.*

S. appeared to have been born with a memory that seemed limitless. If Luria asked S. to recall a list that he had given S. many years ago, S. would first recall that at the time Luria had been wearing a gray shirt; then he would recall the list. He could describe any scene in his mind's eye perfectly because he said he could "see" the person before him in almost hallucinatory detail.

It was clear that S. went about the task of memorizing differently from most people. If given a series of numbers, he said he could "see" the figures in his mind. This is why he didn't care whether he was asked to remember numbers front to back, or vice versa.

His incredible memory did not make for an idyllic life, however. In fact, his life lacked one important feature: because S. relied on factual memory, he was unable to generalize. He couldn't see the forest; he could only count the trees. This is because generalized memory is really the result of an imperfect memory for facts— which S. didn't have. He also had problems with memory chunks, which meant that he was unable to recognize others if they changed subtly, such as by wearing a new suit or getting a haircut. If someone showed up who had shaved off a beard, instead of commenting, "Oh, you've shaved off your beard!" S. was likely to ask, "Oh, have we met?"

Most of us were not born with S.'s unusual memory skills. This doesn't mean that we're fated to drift through life in a haze of absentmindedness, however. It *is* possible to improve your memory for just about every area of your life. What you need to do is learn to use the three keys to a better memory—pay attention, associate, and visualize.

# Key 1. Pay Attention

Simply noticing—paying attention—is the most important thing you can to do to improve your memory. Paying attention involves deciding which things are worth remembering and which can be discarded and forgotten. As generations of students have discovered, no matter how well the material is presented, if you were lost in a daydream when you first heard it, you probably won't remember much of the information later. A lack of attention is also the reason why most people immediately forget a name when first introduced—they're so busy looking at the new person, making initial judgments, and trying to make pleasant conversation, they never really hear the name at all.

If something catches your interest, you'll pay attention; if you're not interested, you just won't have the motivation to concentrate. For most people, paying attention is a conscious effort, not a reflex. Fortunately, even the most diehard daydreamers can learn to improve their ability to pay attention by working at it—in the same way you can to learn to improve anything else.

It's impossible to really pay attention to anything if you're tense, nervous, or under stress. The first thing to do if you want to improve your ability to pay attention is relax. Take a few moments to breathe deeply while consciously relaxing the muscles in the back of your neck and shoulders. This is where a great deal of tension resides.

Whether you're trying to add something to your memory or recall something already in your memory, your desire to be successful will affect your performance. It's important to be calm and *believe* that you can remember. If you start with the idea that it's just too hard to learn something, you're going to have difficulty remembering it later. And if you're convinced that you have a terrible memory, you're putting yourself at a disadvantage when it comes to remembering. It's essential to tell yourself that you *can* remember before you go on to record information.

Everything we perceive is colored by our senses and our emotions. The resulting perceptions are then organized by our reasoning and tucked away in memory. Anyone can absentmindedly observe, but if you really want to remember, you must focus that observation and *concentrate.*

When you are concentrating on something, first ask yourself whether or not you like it—and then ask yourself what it is that you like or don't like. This elaboration is crucial, since you will not remember what you have neglected to elaborate on. When you are really observing and concentrating, you will note expression, composition, color, and mood.

## Understand That Attention Is Fragile

No matter how fine your memory or how powerfully you can focus your attention, the fact remains that the one common denominator in a discussion of attention is its inherent fragility. The average attention span of an audience is only twenty minutes—which is why all good speakers know that they must convey the most important part of their message up front if they are to have an impact on their listeners. Good speakers know that after the first twenty minutes, they will need to employ strategies to hold attention: natural pauses, variation in speed and pitch, good anecdotes, funny stories, or interesting activity.

## Don't Divide Your Attention

Attention can be measured in two ways—how well we avoid distraction and how well we can sustain concentration over a period of time. While humans are usually good at directing their attention to one source, there is evidence that information that isn't attended to is still being analyzed. For example, in the "cocktail party effect" a person who is concentrating on one conversation at a party will likely notice if a nearby conversation suddenly switches to the same topic.

It is possible for humans to do more than one thing at a time. We can eat dinner and watch TV, or talk and drive a car. It seems that as long as the tasks don't depend on the same mental processes, both can be handled at the same time. But if two tasks depend on the same type of mental process (such as listening to a story and reading a book), neither can be accomplished very well. This capacity of being able to pay attention to more than one thing at a time varies from one person to the next, and can be affected by alertness, age, and motivation.

Moreover, even if you could juggle five or six activities at once, it would be impossible to remember much of anything while you were doing it. The best way to remember a fact, an event, or a face is to focus on the information during learning.

## Avoid Distractions

Anticipate your distractions before they occur—think ahead about what is likely to distract you. Remember that the older you get, the harder it is to handle interference. If you have problems concentrating in the workplace, you'll want to eliminate anything that will interfere with your concentration: photos, books, or music, for example. Try using an answering machine to screen phone calls so you won't be tempted to lose track of what you're doing while you're on the phone.

Many drugs that cause drowsiness (sleeping pills, alcohol, etc.) also affect attention and memory. A person's circadian rhythm also influences attention, which is why jet lag can contribute to inattention and resultant memory lapses. Scientists have also discovered that more accidents and judgment errors occur at night.

## Relax

Everyone has experienced the frustration of trying to recall something, only to have it dance on the edge of memory without quite materializing. This phenomenon can be a real problem in retrieving words, and it is a common complaint, especially as we age. Most of the time, a similar word pops into your head instead, which only adds to your frustration. Studies have found that the tip-of-the-tongue phenomenon occurs most often when you try to remember someone's last name, a brand name, or the name of an object. About 50 percent of the time, you will remember the word in less than a minute.

Scientists aren't sure why the tip-of-the-tongue phenomenon occurs, although it may have something to do with an aging retrieval system or metabolic slowdown. These slips occur unpredictably and usually involve words that are rarely used. But there is nothing abnormal about this type of memory lapse.

If you're struggling with this problem, understand that the best chance you have of recalling the word is to *relax.* Instead of wracking your brain to come up with the word, simply shrug and substitute another word. If you act as if the failure to recall the word is not that important, it *becomes* less important physiologically. You can continue to talk about the subject, using synonyms; this should trigger associations that will help put the forgotten word into context. Often, it will suddenly slide into awareness.

If the tip-of-the-tongue phenomenon makes you forget what you came for when you arrive in a room or at the store, try repeating out loud whatever it is you want before you arrive at the location where it is to be found. If you say to yourself, "I'm going to the store to get butter and ice cream," you can prevent yourself from losing track of your mission.

# Key 2. Associate

Mnemonic techniques are the basic tools for improving your attention and thus your memory. Named after Mnemosyne, the Greek goddess of memory, mnemonic techniques are simply methods to improve or develop the memory. They include unusual ways of memorizing huge amounts of information. A number of different techniques are used to associate something you need to be remember with something you already know—first-letter cueing, acronyms, acrostics, popular sayings, etc. Anyone who has ever watched a memory expert mystify his audience is watching a demonstration of what mnemonics can do.

Whether or not we realize it, we all constantly make use of memory-boosting tools. We may use *external* memory aids like the ones we learned about in the first chapter. But it's also possible to train your memory using *internal* memory aids—the mnemonic techniques.

These techniques were of almost unbelievable importance hundreds of years ago, before the invention of printing presses. Because most people didn't have access to pens and paper or printed materials, relying on their own memories was of paramount importance. Indeed, for the ancient Greeks and Romans, mnemonic techniques were one of the most important subjects taught in classical schools. They were often used by the great orators of the time to remember their speeches. Without these techniques, their task would have been impossible.

A mnemonic technique is not just a party trick, but a serious method to help you pay attention, register information, and retrieve information from your memory. The techniques take advantage of the specific ways your brain works and the quirks of memory in order to improve your ability to recall.

Because they're not really tricks, but *methods,* you need to practice them over and over in order to become comfortable with using them every day. These techniques don't rely on magic but on your own ability to visualize, make associations, and organize important information.

# First-Letter Cueing

One of the easiest ways to remember a string of words is to use first-letter cueing, in which the first letter of a word is used as a cue to remember the word itself.

## Acronyms

First-letter cueing usually employs acronyms (making a word out of the first letters of the words to be remembered). For example, to remember the names of the Great Lakes, use the acronym HOMES (Huron, Ontario, Michigan, Erie, and Superior). Many organizations and governmental bodies use acronyms. NATO stands for North Atlantic Treaty Organization, for example, and AA for Alcoholics Anonymous.

Some acronyms become so familiar that we forget what the letters stand for. The word *scuba,* for example, originated as an acronym for Self-Contained Underwater Breathing Apparatus. And *laser* was coined as an acronym for Light Amplification by Stimulated Emission of Radiation.

## Acrostics

A related form of first-letter cueing is the acrostic, in which the first letters in a series of words, lines, or verses form the information to be remembered. For example, to remember the six New England states: Maybe Nobody Visits Mary's Red Car (Maine, New Hampshire, Vermont, Massachusetts, Rhode Island, Connecticut). An acrostic is also the basis for that musical favorite everyone grew up with, Every Good Boy Does Fine, which represents the notes on the lines of the treble clef.

The only problem with acronyms or acrostics is the tendency to forget the system that you devise. To offset this possibility, try making a visual association with the shortcut. To remember the HOMES acronym, picture homes floating on the Great Lakes. When you want to think of their names, the picture of the floating homes will come back to you, and with it the first letter of each lake's name.

Use visual associations. To remember the Great Lakes acronym
"HOMES," visualize homes floating on the Great Lakes.

## Popular Sayings

Whether or not we realize it, each of us uses some of these techniques all the time. Think you don't know any mnemonic techniques? Try again. If you've ever needed to remind yourself whether a month has thirty or thirty-one days, you've probably run through the old chestnut, "Thirty days hath September. . . ." And most people would probably never remember whether to set their clocks ahead or back if it weren't for the saying "Spring forward, fall back."

# Key 3. Visualize

Visualizing is the ability to see a picture in your mind's eye—to see it quite clearly, with color, shape, and form. It's really another word for imagining—imagining with vividness and depth. You imagine—or visualize—in pictures. If you think of a horse, you conjure up an image of a horse; you don't see the word *horse* in letters in your mind (unless you're deliberately trying to visualize the word instead of the animal). Concrete images are always easier to visualize than abstract ideas.

The richness of our imagination allows us to visualize not just the picture of something, but also how it smells, what it feels like, and how it sounds. Thus, it's possible to imagine (or visualize) the softness of a velvet drape, the warmth of a down quilt—it's even possible to catch the whiff of our grandmother's molasses cakes.

Because visualization is so important in using various mnemonic skills, it's something that should be practiced often. The more you practice, the more easily and vividly you'll be able to visualize. Try this:

- Close your eyes, and bring into your mind's eye the image of a cherry pie, just out of the oven.

- Feel the warmth of the pie and sniff the aroma of the cherries.

- Note the brown, crisp crust, the slits for the steam.

- Picture the way the cherry filling has bubbled over the crust, becoming hardened along the edge.

- Now picture yourself cutting into the pie with a knife, removing a slice, and placing it on a plate.

- Watch the cherries slide out from underneath the crust.

- Now visualize yourself getting a bite of pie with your fork.

- Feel the fork slide into the dough and cherries.

- Now you're putting the fork in your mouth. Taste the tart-sweet cherries, the liquid filling, the warm flaky pastry as you chew.

If your mouth has begun to water as you visualized this scene, you've done a good job! Visualization may seem silly to those who aren't accustomed to practicing it, but it underlies all mnemonic techniques. Being able to visualize well can greatly improve your memory skills.

# Practice Visualization

To practice these skills, pick something from the following list each day and practice making it as vivid and real in your mind as you possibly can:

can of soup
raincoat
breakfast
dentist's appointment
new puppy
your desk
chocolate ice-cream soda
pine tree
patchwork quilt

# Be a Good Observer

You may discover that being a good visualizer also means being a good observer. If you haven't spent much time really paying attention to your surroundings, it's not going to be easy to bring them into focus in your mind's eye.

Think that's not your problem? Sit down and try writing an accurate description of the stapler on your desk. Do the same thing with your shoes or your wristwatch. Can you describe them in complete detail? Can you draw a totally accurate picture of them? What exactly does your stapler look like—does it have writing on it? How do the seams of your shoes look? What about the soles and heels? What sort of hands does your watch have? Exercises like these show us that we don't always pay as much attention to our everyday surroundings as we think.

# Improve Your Everyday Memory

P aula was in a hurry to buy a birthday present for her nephew on her way back to work. She pulled into the mall, threw her car into park, and dashed into the closest toy store. When she came out ten minutes later, she scanned the lot and realized with a sinking feeling that she had no idea where she had parked her car. As she ran up and down the lanes, she became even more panicked.

Paula's problem—shared by many people who get lost easily or who can't remember where they have been—is that she didn't pay enough attention to her surroundings when she left her car in the parking lot. Totally absorbed in her errand, she was traveling on "automatic pilot" and had no idea where she was parking. Because of this, she was unable to retrace her steps to her car.

# Everyday Forgetting

There are a host of other types of everyday forgetting. Did you
ever have to return to your house because you couldn't remember
if you turned off the iron, the hair curlers, or the electric heater?
Did you ever lock yourself out of your car or your house? This
type of everyday forgetfulness is very common, partly because
you have done these tasks so often in the past. It can be hard to
remember specifically if you turned off the iron *this time,* as
opposed to all those other times.

Some people are naturally more concerned about "checking,"
and a few, who have an extreme problem in this area, actually
have an obsessive-compulsive disorder. Fortunately, for most
people the urge to check is completely normal.

The busier you are, the more difficult it can be to remember
details—unless you have a system. That's why people on the go
find it so helpful to rely on diaries, lists, calendars, daytimers,
computerized telephone lists, and other memory aids.

There are a variety of practical strategies you can use in your
everyday life to remember the day-to-day details that make your
life run smoothly. These strategies won't give you a photographic
memory, but they will help you avoid those irritating memory
lapses that can cost time, patience, and even money.

# Remembering Places

If you often find yourself in Paula's situation, there are some
simple steps to avoid this problem in the future.

▪ Once you park your car, look around you and record
"cues" to help you find the car. Are you near a telephone
pole? Is there a funny-looking tree nearby?

- *Don't* rely on looking for that distinctive car parked next to you. It almost assuredly will be gone when you try to retrace your steps.

- As you leave your car, turn around to take a "mental photograph" of the scene as you will see it when you come back.

These tips are also useful for remembering where you are going and where you have been when you are traveling or hiking. To better remember your way *as you go:*

- Record visual cues from both directions. You'll be surprised how different things look when seen from the opposite perspective.

- Dwell on strong images as you travel, mentally flashing back to them occasionally.

- Involve as many senses as you can; take note of any unusual smells, noises, etc. The more senses you involve, the stronger the memory will be.

If you don't feel you're very good at following maps, write down directions and study them thoroughly before heading out. There's nothing more stressful than trying to drive and read a list of directions at the same time, and the more stress you're feeling, the harder time you'll have remembering the directions.

In looking at individual differences in memory for places (such as the ability to read a map or find your way in a strange environment), scientists have found that people who have a "good sense of direction" are those who can benefit from experience and acquire an accurate mental map. These individuals also rate themselves as better at giving and following directions and remembering routes as a passenger; they also enjoy reading maps and finding new routes.

If you have a good sense of direction, it may be that you possess a group of abilities (such as good visualization and spatial reasoning) that reinforce each other.

# Remembering Everyday Information

Organize, organize, organize! The more details and information you're trying to juggle—and the more stress you're placing on yourself—the more problems you'll probably have remembering everything you need to do.

## Make To-Do Lists

One of the best-known methods to help us remember important information is the simple "to-do" list. These portable memory aids can help you remember everything from what to buy at the grocery store to what you keep in your safety-deposit box. But making a grocery list won't help you at all if you leave it behind on the kitchen table, or if you can't find it when you need it because of the clutter in your purse or your briefcase.

■ Always keep your lists in one place, where they can be easily located.

■ Organize your list into categories. If you're making a grocery list, group similar foods together: vegetables and fruit, meat, frozen foods, etc. If you're good at visualizing, think of the store as you write the list, and place the items in order depending on which aisles you'll visit first. If you've got coupons, organize them in the same fashion. It's much easier to check off items as you purchase them than it would be if you wrote everything down in no particular order.

- Make your lists easy to find. Don't scribble a long list on a matchbook-sized scrap of paper; you'll be sure to misplace it. Find a large piece of paper—preferably colored, to make it stand out. Some people find it helpful to write a grocery list on the back of an envelope and to carry their coupons inside the envelope.

# Record Important Numbers

Because you'll never know when you're going to need important numbers, it's a good idea to keep them where you'll be sure to find them. By always keeping them in the same place, you'll be sure to locate them even if you're rushed or under great stress. Be sure to keep these numbers in your wallet or purse:

- phone numbers of your doctors, contact person in case of an emergency, close friend or neighbor, and your home
- medical insurance number
- Social Security number
- license plate number

# Make Packing Lists

Whether you're taking a trip or moving across town, packing lists will come in handy. To make sure you don't leave an important item behind, make a packing list before you take any trip. Some experts suggest starting at one end of the body and working your way up or down, to avoid missing any important item of clothing. Others suggest grouping clothes according to type (good clothes, casual clothes, sports clothes, and so on). Be sure to include medication, equipment, and personal-care items:

- As you pack each item, check it off on your list.

- After you've finished packing, place the list on top of your suitcase so you can add to it as you remember items.

- Keep the list stored in the suitcase so you can check off items as you repack. This way, you'll never leave your favorite expensive shampoo or your toothbrush behind in somebody else's bathroom!

When you pack for a move, it's important to keep a list for each container so you'll know where everything is. Otherwise, you're sure to need an item immediately and have no clue as to where it might be found. Make a list of items as each box is packed, and place the list on top of the contents before you close the lid. To avoid having to open a whole series of boxes just to find your can opener once the boxes have arrived in the new house, number each box and keep a list of numbered containers and their general contents. Or simply number the lists to match the numbered boxes and keep the lists with you.

# Plan Ahead for Medical Visits

If you know you're going to be visiting the doctor in a week or so, write down a list of questions that you want to ask. Most people find visiting the doctor to be stressful, and some are so intimidated by medical settings that every question they wanted to ask simply vanishes. Write the questions in your list starting with the most important ones and ending with the least important (in case you don't get through them all).

- What is the name of the illness?

- What causes it?

- What can be done to alleviate symptoms?

- What treatments are available?

- What is the cost of treatment?

- Where are treatments available?

- Are there any experimental treatments available?
- If so, how does one join the trials?
- What medications are necessary?
- Should the medicine be taken at any particular time of day?
- Can the medication interact with other pills, food, or beverages?

If you have any sort of continuing medical problem—especially if you visit several specialists or take many medications—it's a good idea to keep a medical notebook to take with you to all of your appointments. In this notebook, you should record your medical history, including dates of all surgeries, medical visits, tests ordered and their results, medications, etc. Such a notebook is invaluable when you are asked to fill out questionnaires for new physicians, and it can help your doctors trace your medical history and gain insight into your condition.

# Keeping Track of Dates and Appointments

David was a very happily married man who was incapable of remembering the date of his wedding anniversary. He knew the date fell in April, sometime during the last two weeks, but beyond that he was totally unable to recall the day. He spent a great deal of time worrying about why he had so much trouble with this particular memory.

If you've ever been chagrined to realize you've forgotten an important birthday or anniversary, you know how vital it can be to remember dates that are important to your friends and family. In fact, remembering dates is one of the most common memory problems, but it's nothing to be too concerned about. Using mental strategies and mechanical reminders, it's possible to conquer this particular memory lapse.

# Carry a Notebook

Whenever you're away from home, carry a small notebook with you to jot down things to do and important appointments. It should fit into your purse, briefcase, or glove compartment, and it should be big enough so you can write down brief essential information that you'll then transfer to your calendar at home.

# Use a Calendar

A notebook or calendar with names and birth dates can be very helpful. Jane, who has great trouble remembering to buy and mail cards, keeps a special calendar with all important dates marked. At the beginning of each year, she goes to the store and buys all the cards she needs for the entire year. She addresses and stamps all the envelopes and files each card between the pages of the corresponding month. As each month passes, she flips the page and writes out notes for each person who's having a special day that month. She usually stocks up on a few extra cards for unexpected weddings, baby showers, and funerals.

At home, you can keep a weekly or monthly calendar to write down all of your engagements from your portable appointment notebook and anything from your to-do list that needs to be recorded. It's best if you can do this at the same time every day—for example, right after dinner in the evening—so that you'll make it a habit. Anything you want to remember, no matter how seemingly unimportant—from doctor's appointments to grooming the cat—should be written down on this calendar.

Every morning, check this calendar, and then cross off each task as you accomplish it during the day. At the end of the day, you can transfer anything left undone onto the next day's space.

When you buy a new calendar at the beginning of each year, transfer all the important dates from the old calendar so you will have an automatic agenda for the new year.

Using a calendar can be very effective, but you must keep up with it. Be sure to keep the calendar in one place so you can always find it—a desk or hall table works well. Some people prefer magnetic calendars that they can keep on the refrigerator. And make sure you always transfer needed dates from your portable notebook.

This system can be very effective in helping you remember everyday appointments and important dates, because it helps you organize information and manage time. Because you're writing down and transferring information, it forces you to pay attention to what you want to remember—and paying attention is the very best way to remember anything. As you write down the information, you're "rehearsing" it, which will also help you remember.

## Check Your Calendar Weekly

At the beginning of each week, check your calendar for any important dates or appointments that you want to remember. To be effective, you must do this every week. If you start skipping, you will inevitably skip a week that contains an important date you needed to remember.

If there is a particular date that you have trouble remembering, say it out loud. Anticipate the date and make a comment about it, out loud, as often as possible.

## Make Visual Cues

As the date approaches, make some visual cues that you won't miss. Place a note on the steering wheel of your car or on the receiver of your telephone. Insert a colored piece of paper in your briefcase so that one end protrudes. Leave a note to yourself on the seat of your office chair. Put one in your shoes, your handbag, or your wallet. Don't assume you will remember—leave plenty of cues to jog your memory.

# Conquering Absentmindedness

If you're the type of person who can never find your glasses, your car keys, or your wallet, it's probably because you're absent-minded and easily distracted. You just haven't been paying attention when you put these items down, and failure to pay attention is the primary problem behind absentmindedness.

You're most likely to be absentminded when you're engaged in a regular routine in a familiar environment, or when you are distracted or preoccupied so that your attention is elsewhere. For this reason, developing a habit of putting things where they belong will help your memory. This way, even when you're not paying attention you'll be able to find the items, because you can assume that you've automatically put the item where it belongs.

This is a common problem for daydreamers. They tend not to care what is happening around them, or they are easily distracted and vulnerable to interference. They may always be thinking about other things, or about things that they want to do later, neglecting to pay attention to the here and now.

If you complain about being absentminded or having memory lapses, you're probably more concerned about your failure to do something you wanted to do rather than not being able to remember information from the past. That's because we tend to feel that if we can't remember something from the past, we just have an unreliable memory. But if we can't remember to do things in the future, we run the risk of being considered personally unreliable.

# Remember Routine Tasks

Many people have trouble remembering habitual tasks, such as brushing their teeth, taking a vitamin pill, or locking the door before going to bed. This problem results from not paying attention while performing the task. If you do forget to pay attention when turning off the stove or unplugging the iron as you leave the house, you may need to take a quick trip back home to check.

If you forget habitual tasks, the key to solving your problem is to relate the activity to something that you won't forget to do every day. If you've been forgetting to brush your teeth in the morning, then tell yourself that each morning you won't eat breakfast until you brush your teeth. By incorporating a task into an outline of things you *don't* forget to do (such as eat breakfast), you're less likely to forget that task.

It's a fact that the more organized and routine your life, the less risk you will run of forgetting anything. This is why older people often have less of a problem with absentmindedness than younger folks; their lives rely far more on a daily routine.

# Remember Occasional Tasks

While many people have problems with habitual tasks, the real problem that concerns most absentminded people is forgetting tasks that come up only once in a while. Forgetting to take your vitamin pill one day will most likely not have serious consequences, but forgetting to mail an IRS payment can cause real problems.

Here are a few suggestions that will help you remember occasional tasks:

- Make a list of what you need to do, and check it frequently.

- Visualize something that is related to the task and associate it with what you need to do. (Picture the IRS payment with a big smile, sitting on top of the mailbox.)

- Use memory aids, including timers, calendars, appointment books, and string or a rubber band on your hand.

## Get the Time Right

Simply remembering that you need to do something in the future isn't good enough if you haven't remembered at the right time. For example, if you remember a week before you should mail your IRS payment that you need to do it, but then forget all about the task until the deadline has passed, you haven't solved the problem.

One way to avoid this difficulty is to cue your attention at the right time. For example, you might take the IRS payment and physically place it on the table by the front door—or tape it to the front door if you are concerned you might overlook it on the table. If you're squeamish about taping IRS envelopes to doors, you can substitute a symbolic reminder: tape a dollar bill or stick a Post-it note to the front door. The sight of that green bill or yellow paper on the door should be enough to trigger your memory that something needs to be done that day.

Here are some other memory cues you can try:

- Place a rubber band around your wrist.

- Move your engagement ring to your right hand.

- Take off your watch, or put it on your opposite wrist.

- Attach a safety pin to the inside of the sleeve of your shirt or dress.

The profoundly absentminded may worry that a symbolic cue isn't straightforward enough to help them remember. Was the

Remember tasks like mailing a tax return by creating
an amusing mental picture.

rubber band to remind them to buy rubber bands or take out the trash? If this is a concern, you can take the symbolic cue one step further and add a visualizing step to the process. If you want to remember to mail that IRS envelope and you put a rubber band around your wrist, then picture yourself dropping the rubber band into the mailbox. Or imagine crumpling up your payment and shooting it via the rubber band at the mailbox.

# Remember What You're Doing

Another kind of absentmindedness occurs when you go into a room to get something and then forget why you're there. While this is one memory lapse that causes some people to truly worry about their sanity, it is actually quite common. Estimates suggest that more than half of all people experience this problem. It's simply caused by a lack of attention that can be easily remedied.

Every time a thought occurs to you to go into a room to get something, simply stop for a moment and say to yourself (or out loud, if you have a real problem with this) why you are going into the other room. If you find yourself standing in the room without any idea why you are there, try retracing your steps to where you were when you had the thought to leave the room. This form of association will often help bring your errand back to mind.

# Improve Your Awareness

The key to understanding how to cure absentmindedness is to become profoundly aware of what you are doing. Here's how:

1. Pause.

2. Focus your mind.

3. Anticipate your distractions.

4. Take immediate action.

# Pause to Remember

The first step in becoming aware is to pause before doing something you want to remember. Before going to bed or out the door, ask yourself, "Where am I going? What do I need to do?" Stop wherever you are, breathe deeply to slow down, and take the time to think. If you're locking your car, stop and think about what you're doing. Watch yourself as you slip the key into the lock, turn it, remove the key, and put it in your pocket.

If you often find yourself losing your car in a parking lot, as soon as you park pause briefly to record visual cues to help you remember the place. Associate the car with a permanent cue—a tall tree, a street lamp, or a certain scene.

## Focus Your Mind

Next, concentrate on what you are doing. Consciously focus your mind on your task. Speak out loud to force yourself to attend to what you are doing. If you frequently forget to turn off the stove, make it a regular routine to go into the kitchen and slowly survey the appliances. As you look at each one, say out loud: "The oven is turned off. The stove burners are turned off. The toaster oven is turned off. The coffee pot is unplugged." By speaking out loud, you are using not only your mind, but your eyes, ears, and voice to reinforce your attention. Now when you're driving down the freeway and you suddenly ask yourself whether or not the electric frying pan is turned off, you will remember quite clearly that it is.

If you find yourself leaving important items behind—your parking pass, your purse, your sunglasses—establish a routine before leaving the house each morning similar to the appliance drill. Line up every item you will need that day, and then, out loud, go through each one, using each of your senses. Check your appointment calendar to see what stops you'll be making, and assure yourself that everything you need to take with you is lined up and ready to go in the hallway before you depart.

If your problem is locking your keys in the car, you can use the same techniques to focus your mind. First, each time you park the car say out loud, "I am removing the keys," as you take the keys from the ignition. Tell yourself that you are putting the keys in your pocket as you do so, and before you lock the car use your voice again to double-check that the keys are safely in your purse, pocket, or wallet. If you still have problems—or you just don't like worrying—keep a spare car key in your purse or in a magnetic box under the hood of the car.

## Anticipate Your Distractions

Think ahead to minimize whatever is likely to distract you. For example, if you're in a hurry, you're tired, under stress, anxious, depressed or you have a problem with automatic gestures, you're going to have a harder time paying attention and therefore, you will probably have a hard time staying in focus and remembering important details.

## Take Immediate Action

Do it now, while you're thinking of it. Must you take a video back to the library? Mail that important letter? Put the video or the letter by the front door now. If you can avoid procrastinating, you can avoid many types of forgetfulness.

# Remembering Quantities

Have you ever been in the midst of baking a cake and not been able to remember how many cups of flour you've already added? Or has someone interrupted you and made you lose track while you were counting spoonfuls of coffee?

To avoid this problem, try visualizing the quantity of flour or coffee in the measure, and pour it in while saying to yourself the quantity you are using and looking at it intently. Actually seeing the amount, and commenting on it out loud, will be easier to remember than abstract numbers. Going through the motions triggers kinesthetic memory, and when you comment on those motions, you reinforce the memory trace.

You can also use a backup strategy. For every cup of flour you pour into the bowl, set aside one raisin (or spoon, or spice jar). Each time you add another cup of flour, set aside another raisin on the counter. Then you will be able to check visually exactly how many cups you've added, even if you are interrupted several times.

# Recalling Where You Put Things

If you have trouble remembering where you put things, the solution is to put everything back where it belongs, all the time. This way, you won't ever have to wonder where you put your glasses, your keys, or the TV remote. Take an inventory of your home right now. Find a specific place to keep:

- glasses
- keys
- medications
- letters to be answered
- bills to be paid
- safety-deposit-box key
- important papers
- coupons
- TV remote

If you can't find things because you haven't paid attention when you put them down, there's a good strategy for locating them—it's the old "retrace your steps" ploy. Think back to what you were doing that led up to the act you're trying to recall.

# Keeping to Schedules

You'll be better able to keep your life on schedule if you remember some basic routines—routines to pay bills, take medications, or do daily tasks.

## Pay Your Bills

Do you pay all your bills in an orderly fashion, or do they pile up on your desk until dunning notices start to appear? Whether you pay bills once a month or every week, you'll need a place to keep your bills until you pay them. Try putting them all in a file folder, or designate one desk drawer just for bills. When a bill comes in, throw it immediately into the folder or drawer. Keep your checkbook there, too; that way, when bill-paying time rolls around, everything will be waiting in one place.

## Schedule Your Chores

It's not hard to figure out when to do the dishes or wash the clothes, but for those chores that aren't done every day or even every week it helps to schedule a specific time. Associating chores that are only done once or twice a year with a specific holiday can often help.

Because so many people can never remember when they last changed the battery in their smoke detectors, fire departments have realized that linking a battery change with the twice-a-year shift between standard time and daylight-savings time would be an excellent way for everyone to remember to change their batteries as they reset their clocks. This strategy also works well with other occasional chores, such as vacuuming the coils in your refrigerator, cleaning the filter in your heater or air conditioner, or vacuuming the lint from your dryer.

## Use a Timer

For those who have trouble remembering specific duties around the house, a simple kitchen timer can work wonders. For example, when wash day comes, some people can never remember to make the trips to the laundry room to put in water softener and take out a load of wash from the dryer to put in a new load. By setting a timer to ring fifteen minutes after putting in the wash, you can remind yourself to get there in time to pour in the softener.

Timers can also be used to remind you when a favorite TV show is on, to make a phone call at a particular time, or to remember when to leave home to pick up your child at the babysitter's.

# Thinking Up Your Own Strategies

These are just a few of the many ways that simple everyday strategies can be used to help you remember important details around the house. If you have trouble remembering something—*anything* —the solution is simply to *pay attention* and *act deliberately* to impress the information in your mind.

# Learn the Method of Loci

The oldest known mnemonic strategy (it dates to 500 B.C.)
is the method of loci (*loci* is the plural of *locus*, which means
place or location). This method is based on the assumption that people best remember familiar locations. Therefore,
these locations can serve as clues to help remember information
associated with them.

To use the method of loci effectively, all you do is link something you want to remember with a location. When you want
to recall the information, you simply remember the location.

According to Cicero, this method was developed by a poet
named Simonides of Ceos, who was the only survivor of a building collapse during a dinner at which he had been speaking.
Simonides was able to identify the dead, who were crushed

beyond recognition, by his recollection of where the guests had been sitting at the table. Because he was able to remember everyone's name by visualizing where they had been sitting, he realized that a person's memory probably could be improved by associating mental images of locations for each item to be remembered.

The loci system was used as a memory tool by both Greek and Roman orators, who took advantage of the technique to speak without notes. They would visualize objects that represented the topics they wanted to discuss, and then mentally place the objects in different locations within a building. As an orator spoke, he would mentally move through the building, retrieving the imaginary objects from each location as he came to it. This ancient oratorical method is the origin of our idiom "in the first place." The method of loci was the most popular mnemonic system until about the middle of the 1600s, when other strategies (such as the phonetic and peg systems) were introduced.

# Following in the Footsteps of Memory

The method of loci is easy to learn, and it works very well for people who are good at visualizing. Here's how you start:

- Choose a place you know well, such as your house.

- Visualize a series of locations in that place in a logical order. For example, begin at your front door, go through the hall, turn into the living room, proceed through the dining room and into the kitchen. As you enter each location, always move logically and consistently in the same direction, from one side of the room around to the other. Each piece of furniture or architectural element of the house can serve as an additional location.

- When you want to remember information, you'll associate each piece of information in the order it is to be remembered with a particular location in the house.

Say you want to remember your shopping list:
    Typing paper
    Onions
    Carrots
    Hamburger
    Ice cream

As you visualize your front door, imagine typing paper plastered all over the door. Don't just imagine the words *typing paper*—really see the paper, pure white sheets pasted all over your oak door. Now open the door and enter the hall, where you see a huge Bermuda onion sitting on the steps in your front hall, sipping an iced tea. Now turn into the living room, and visualize a six-foot carrot wearing a red beret standing by the fireplace. Sitting in a chair by the fireplace is a giant Big Mac (hamburger), and the Big Mac is licking a strawberry ice-cream cone.

When you want to remember your shopping list, all you have to do is to visualize your front door. You will instantly see typing paper. As you enter the front hall, the Bermuda onion will pop into your mind. The more outrageous and unusual you make your images, the easier you will find it is to remember them.

This method can be used for a variety of lists, for speeches, names, things to do—even to remember a thought you want to keep in mind. If you're mowing the lawn and you suddenly want to remember to tell your sister the funny story about your next-door neighbor's dog, simply picture the dog doing something funny in your living room. When you're talking to your sister and you want to remember the story, simply visualize your living room and the image of the dog will come back.

To use the method of loci to remember a grocery list, picture each item in a different part of your house. The more outrageous the mental image, the easier you'll remember it!

# Expanding Your Loci System

The loci system works so well because it alters the way you remember. It allows you to use familiar locations to cue yourself about things you want to recall. Because the locations are organized in a natural order, one memory easily leads into the next, dragging with it whatever information you have attached to the location.

You can enlarge the system by adding other buildings you know well: your school or office building, a store, your parents' house. Of course, you don't *have* to visualize a house. You could just as easily walk through a neighborhood, take a trip downtown, or visualize your garden, if those areas are well known to you. You can even use parts of your own body, if you wish.

When the loci method was first revived, students were instructed to keep the locations widely spaced. However, research has shown that it is more important for the loci to be visually distinct. It's also important to form a strong association between each item and its location—have the item *interact* with its location in some compelling way. This is the only way the locations will be effective in helping you retrieve information.

It's also possible to add more than one item to any one location. For example, if you have a list of fifty items to purchase at the store, you could theoretically place five items at each of ten locations. It is unlikely, however, that you could remember the five items in any particular order at each location. Ideally, each of the five items should interact at each of the ten locations.

The method of loci was often used by S., the Russian newspaper reporter described earlier in this book. As Luria reported in his book, *Mind of a Mnemonist:*

> When S. read through a long series of words, each word
> would elicit a graphic image. And since the series was
> fairly long, he had to find some way of distributing these

*images in a mental row or sequence. Most often . . . he would "distribute" them along some roadway or street he visualized in his mind. . . . Frequently he would take a mental walk along that street . . . and slowly make his way down, "distributing" his images at houses, gates and in store windows. This technique of converting a series of words into a series of graphic images explains why S. could so readily reproduce a series from start to finish or in reverse order; how he could rapidly name the word that preceded or followed one I'd selected from the series. To do this he would simply begin his walk, either from the beginning or end of the street, find the image of the object I had named and "take a look at" whatever happened to be situated on either side of it.*

# Follow the Link Method

The link method, also known as the chain system, is the most basic of the mnemonic strategies. It's used for memorizing short lists of items, such as a shopping list, in which each item is linked to the next. Here's how to perform the link system:

- Form a visual image for each item in the list.

- Associate the image for the first item with the image for the second item.

- Associate the image for the third item with the image for the second item, and so on.

- Begin with the first item and proceed in order as each item leads to the next one to recall the list.

It's important not to try to associate every item with every other item. Instead, you're just associating the items two at a time. Here's a sample grocery list that can be easily remembered using the link method:

> Milk
> Eggs
> Pork chops
> Syrup
> Peas

First you would form a visual association between milk and eggs. Perhaps you might imagine an egg trying to cram itself into a glass milk bottle. Next, create a link between eggs and pork chops. Maybe the image of a giant egg waltzing with a pig would do the trick. To associate pork chops with syrup, imagine a pig dipping his leg into a pool of maple syrup.

While you're creating your visual associations, make sure you really see them vividly in your mind's eye. Although a funny or unusual association is good, what's most important is that you use the first association that comes to your mind, since this will make it easier for you to remember that same association.

# The Limitations of Links

You may have already spotted one of the problems with this system—each item is linked to the previous one, except for the very first item. You'll need to think of some way to cue that first item. If the list is a shopping list, try linking the first item with the entryway to the store. If the list was given to you by somebody else, link the first item with that person.

It's also possible that if you forget one item on the linked list, the item that it is linked with next may also be forgotten. The method of loci has an advantage over the link system in that even

To use the link method to remember to buy milk, eggs, pork chops, and maple syrup, create mental images associating each item with the next.

if one item is forgotten, it will not affect memory for the next item, because all of the items are linked to an unforgettable place, not to each other.

Both the link and loci methods can be used to remember items in order. However, neither of these memory techniques allows you to locate just one particular item on the list. For example, if you wanted to find the tenth item on your list, in the link system you would have to work your way through the first nine items in your list to get to it. Likewise, in the loci method, you would have to walk through your house step by step until you arrived at the tenth item. On the other hand, this weakness is true of most lists that we have thoroughly learned in a serial way. It's much easier to recite the letters of the alphabet in order than to name them all in a random sequence.

Aware of this problem, the ancients did come up with one way around it when using the method of loci. Every so often—say, every fifth location—place a distinguishing mark. At the fifth location, for example, picture a five-dollar bill. At the tenth location, visualize a clock with its hands pointing to ten o'clock. This way, if for some reason you want to find the eleventh item, you have only to visualize the tenth location quickly, and then you can move ahead one to the eleventh. This same strategy can be used with linking—link a $5 bill between the fourth and sixth link.

# Practicing Linking

If you can use the link method successfully with ten items, you can use it to remember twenty or thirty things, too. There's really no limit to the number of items you can remember with this system. Before going any further, try this system out. Have someone give you ten concrete words (not verbs or adjectives) and write them down as they are called out. Writing them down will enable the other person to check your responses, and it will give you a brief amount of time to think of links. Whatever the first word is, associate it with the person. If the first word is *horse,* imagine seeing a horse sitting on the person's head. That's all it should take to get you started in immediately recalling the words.

Now practice with a few links of your own devising, gradually lengthening the lists. Once you get really comfortable with this method, you can try it out with verbs or adjectives, too.

# The Story System

A close cousin to the link system is the story system, in which each item in a list is linked to the one after it by an interconnected story. For example, to remember the list given on page 50, you could create a story like this:

> *The milk bottle picked up an egg to throw at the pig (pork chops), who slipped in a pool of syrup and slid into a pea patch.*

The story system is different from the link method in that each of the items is linked in an integrated narrative. This logical sequence may be easier for people to recall than a list of simple but unrelated paired associations. On the other hand, the story system can take more time, because you have to fit all the items into the story. The story system becomes progressively more difficult as the length of the list grows. It doesn't really matter how many items there are in the link method. And, unlike with the story method, you can recall a link-method list either backward or forward.

# How Effective Are the Link and Story Systems?

Scientists who have studied the link and story systems have found that both systems can help people learn and remember word lists. In fact, there is evidence that those who learn the link system can remember up to three times as much as those who do not learn the technique. Research has also revealed that the story method is effective with abstract words (although slightly less effective than with concrete words), and that unrelated sentences can be remembered better when they were strung together as a story.

Both methods have also been shown to be more effective than the use of imagery or rehearsal alone. When the order of recall was important, the superiority of these mnemonic techniques was even greater.

# Master the Peg System

**P**eg systems are probably among the best known of all the memory systems. The use of peg words is a type of mnemonic strategy in which items to be remembered are mentally *pegged* to (associated with) certain images in a prearranged order.

The peg method is superior to both the link and loci methods because it is not dependent on sequential retrieval. You can access any item on the list without having to work your way through all the items before it.

There are a number of similarities between the peg and the loci methods. In both, items to be remembered are associated with previously memorized concrete items, thus creating a sort of mental filing system. Peg words in the peg method and locations in the loci method are used in the same fashion, and both peg words and locations can be used over and over again. Recall is also similar for both—you move through the house, or along your list of peg words, and retrieve information.

# What Is the Peg System?

The peg system is a memory technique in which a standard set of peg words (concrete nouns) are learned, and items to be remembered are linked to the pegs with visual imagery. The system can be traced to the mid-1600s, when it was developed by Henry Herdson, who linked a digit with any one of several objects that resembled the number (for example, 1 = candle; 3 = trident).

The system got its name from the fact that peg words act as mental pegs or hooks on which a person "hangs" the information that needs to be remembered. It is probably one of the most famous mnemonic devices, popular with entertainers and students of memory training. The peg words help organize material that needs to be remembered, and act as reminders to recall that material.

A number of studies have shown that people are able to use the peg system effectively on lists up to forty words long. It can also be used to help form concepts in tasks requiring high memory demands, remembering ideas, and similar applications. Peg words are helpful in remembering lists for shopping or errands, in organizing activities, and in giving people a sense of being in control of their lives.

There are a number of different peg systems, all of which use a concrete object to represent each number. The difference lies in the various ways to choose the object that represents each number. The systems include the rhyming method, the look-alike method, and the meaning method. Most peg systems don't include a peg word for zero, but you can invent your own. The rhyming

method could use 0 = hero; the look-alike method could use 0 =
cookie, and the meaning method could use 0 = box (empty box).

# The Rhyming-Peg Method

The best-known peg method was introduced in England in 1879
by John Sambrook. It is known as the rhyming-peg method because numbers from one to ten are associated with rhymes: one-
bun, two-shoe, etc. In order to use this system, you must first
memorize the words that rhyme with numbers one through ten:

One is a bun   *S U N*
Two is a shoe
Three is a tree
Four is a door
Five is a hive
Six are sticks
Seven is heaven
Eight is a gate
Nine is a vine   *n D IN LE*
Ten is a hen

Most people already know many of these associations from
nursery rhymes they learned as children. Now, as you say each
rhyme, visualize the item that the peg word represents. Picture it
vividly—is the bun a sesame seed hamburger bun? A hot cross
bun? Is the shoe an elegant high heel or a peasant's muddy clog?

Now draw the item on a piece of paper. The act of drawing will
help you remember the rhyme. (You'll remember it better if you
draw it for the same reason that you remember directions better if
you're the driver rather than the passenger in a car. The act of
driving forces you to pay attention in a way that simply riding
along does not.)

When learning the rhyming method, imagine each peg word as vividly as possible. The bun should be a sesame seed bun, a hot cross bun, or a toasted and buttered bun. The tree should also be specific—an oak, a spindly pine, a silver birch.

By visualizing the object that each word represents, you will fix it securely in your mind, creating a strong mental association between the numbers and the words that rhyme with them. Because of this visualization, this system is also known as a visual peg system—a type of visual imagery method.

Once you have formed an association between the numbers and the words that rhyme with them, you've constructed your pegs. Practice by saying each of the peg words aloud. Now try "seeing" the peg words for numbers as you jump around—five, three, eight, one, four. Because the words rhyme with the numbers, you don't have to say the numbers to remember the words.

Now, if you want to remember a list, all you have to do is link each item with a peg—the first with a bun, the second with a shoe, the third with a tree, and so on. To remember the list, call up the pegs and the mental images that are linked to the pegs will be recalled automatically.

Here's how you would remember the ten items on the following grocery list:

> peas
> pork chops
> milk
> bread
> eggs
> butter
> tomatoes
> soap
> peanut butter
> Swiss cheese

Attach each item on the list to one of the rhyming words, making the association as vivid and ridiculous as possible. Don't be literal; make your images as silly and exaggerated as you can. The more absurd the associations, the more easily they will be remembered.

Try visualizing the first item (peas) wearing leotards, tap dancing on a bun. Think of pork chops as a pig in tennis shoes. To remember milk, imagine bottles of milk hanging from an apple tree. The loaf of bread could be visualized knocking on the front door, wearing sunglasses and a pith helmet. Imagine eggs with wings, flying around a beehive. Butter could be impaled on sticks and held melting over a campfire. Tomatoes are next; visualize them splattering against the portals of heaven in a vain attempt at entry. Picture Tom Sawyer scrawling Becky's name in soap on the front gate at Aunt Polly's house. Jars of peanut butter could be growing on a vine, and to remember Swiss cheese, picture a giant Rhode Island Red hen running around with a block of holey cheese in its mouth.

Now, when you think of a bun you see the peas. When you think of shoes, you picture the pig in tennis shoes, and so on. The peg words can be used over and over—with each new list, the previous words will be erased. Each peg is a clue to an association with the item to be remembered, and to recall the item, all that has to be remembered is the peg.

Peg words can help you remember lists of items or errands. They can be invaluable in helping you organize all of your daily activities.

This visual peg method may not work for patients with memory problems caused by brain damage on one side, as it requires remembering in two distinct stages, one involving the right hemisphere and the other involving the left.

To use the peg method to remember a grocery list, create a mental image associating each item with the corresponding peg rhyme. If item #1 is a can of peas, associate it with "one is a bun."

# Alphabet Pegs

Numbers make a good peg system because they are naturally ordered and everyone knows them. For this reason, the alphabet also makes a good peg system. Peg words can be created that rhyme with, or sound similar to, the letters of the alphabet they represent:

| | | |
|---|---|---|
| *a* = hay | *j* = jay | *s* = ass |
| *b* = bee | *k* = quay | *t* = tea |
| *c* = sea | *l* = elbow | *u* = you |
| *d* = deed | *m* = hem | *v* = me |
| *e* = eve | *n* = den | *w* = double you |
| *f* = effort | *o* = bow | *x* = axe |
| *g* = gee | *p* = pea | *y* = why |
| *h* = age | *q* = cue | *z* = zebra |
| *i* = eye | *r* = oar | |

Or, you can construct peg words without any rhymes, using the letters of the alphabet to begin each word:

| | | |
|---|---|---|
| *a* = apple | *j* = jelly | *s* = snake |
| *b* = boy | *k* = kangaroo | *t* = tire |
| *c* = can | *l* = lamp | *u* = umbrella |
| *d* = dog | *m* = mask | *v* = vase |
| *e* = elephant | *n* = needle | *w* = wing |
| *f* = fish | *o* = orangutan | *x* = xylophone |
| *g* = goat | *p* = pony | *y* = yak |
| *h* = horse | *q* = queen | *z* = zebra |
| *i* = igloo | *r* = rat | |

You can use alphabet peg words in the same way as you use number peg words, but they can't be directly retrieved quite so easily, because most people don't know the numerical value of the letters of the alphabet.

# Other Peg Systems

As we noted earlier, peg words can also be selected on the basis of meaning: 1 = me (there is only one me); 3 = pitchfork (three prongs); 5 = hand (five fingers). This system is limited, however, in that it is hard to find good peg words to represent numbers beyond ten. Some people also use a look-alike system, choosing peg words that represent objects that look like the numbers:

  1  = pen
  2  = swan
  8  = hourglass
 10  = knife and plate

# Phonetic Pegs

The phonetic peg system is more flexible than the rhyming system because it allows for more than ten or twenty peg words while still retaining the peg system's benefits of direct retrieval. However, it is also more complex and requires more study and effort to master.

Also referred to as the number-to-sound system, the phonetic peg system is a good way to remember numbers, because it allows you to make them more meaningful. In this system, each number is represented by a consonant sound, which is combined with vowels to code numbers into words.

When it was introduced in 1648, the digits were represented by letters of the alphabet, both consonants and vowels. The system was refined in 1813 so that the digits were represented only by consonants selected for their similarity to or association with the digits they represented.

Mnemonists in the 1800s tinkered with the system further until it reached its present form as a representation of consonant sounds. For example, 0 = *z* (the first sound in *zero*), and 1 = *t* (because both 1 and *t* have one downstroke).

| Digit | Consonant sound | Memory aid |
|-------|-----------------|------------|
| 1 | *t, d, th* | *t* has one downstroke |
| 2 | *n* | two downstrokes |
| 3 | *m* | three downstrokes |
| 4 | *r* | last sound of the word *four* |
| 5 | *l* | Roman numeral for 50 is L |
| 6 | *j, sh, ch*, soft *g* | reversed script *J* looks like 6 |
| 7 | *k, q*, hard *c*, hard *g* | *k* is made of two 7s back to back |
| 8 | *f, v* | script *f* looks like an 8 |
| 9 | *p, b* | *p* is the reversed image of 9 |
| 0 | *z, s*, soft *c* | *z* is the first letter of zero |

In the phonetic system, consonant sounds are important, not the consonants themselves. This is why similar-sounding consonants are grouped together (except for 2, 3, 4, and 5). It's an important distinction, since the same letter can take on different sounds (for example, *ch* can spell *church* and *chemical*) and different letters can take on the same sound (*sugar* and *ocean*).

The primary letter for each digit is listed first. You can remember the others by learning these simple acrostics:

1 = tarries through dinner

6 = Jean should change gems

7 = king quits cooking goat meat

8 = fun vacuuming

9 = peanut butter

0 = zebras sip cider

A repeated consonant that makes only one sound is written digitally only once (*little* would be expressed as 515, not 5115), but a repeated letter with two different sounds has both sounds included (*accent* would be expressed as 7021).

After you have learned all the consonant sounds for each digit, you can use this system in several ways. You can construct words to file away in your memory, much the way you did with the loci and other peg systems. You can also encode any numbers into words to make them easier to learn.

To construct words, begin by assigning a peg word that begins with the consonant represented by the digit. Two-digit numbers are represented by a peg word that begins with a consonant sound representing the first digit and ends with a consonant sound representing the second digit.

| | |
|---|---|
| 1 = tie | 11 = tent |
| 2 = not | 12 = tin |
| 3 = man | 13 = tomtom |
| 4 = rat | 14 = tire |
| 5 = lamb | 15 = towel |
| 6 = jelly | 16 = tush |
| 7 = key | 17 = tack |
| 8 = finger | 18 = taffy |
| 9 = pie | 19 = top |
| 10 = toes | 20 = nose |

While many people consider the phonetic system too cumbersome and difficult to bother to learn, it has been used successfully with brain-damaged patients. In at least one study, four out of seven patients with severe verbal-memory problems were helped to learn experimental material and practical information with the system, although it took a long time to learn. Others believe that the system may be of some help to those with mild head injuries, but would probably not help those with more severe memory impairments.

# Remember Names

ue was circulating at a New Year's Eve party when a tall
man with a familiar face appeared at her elbow. Obviously
recognizing her, he starting talking about Sue's job at a large publishing firm. Sue did remember that he was an author, and agreed
to send a copy of her firm's new publication list to the address he
gave her. As she took out a pen, she realized to her embarrass-
ment that she couldn't recall his last name—but since they had
been talking for about ten minutes, she didn't want to admit that
she had forgotten.

As she hesitated, she hit on a way to alleviate her embar-
rassment. "And how do you spell your last name?" she asked
innocently, pencil poised. He looked at her, puzzled, and then
slowly spelled out:

"S-M-I-T-H."

We've all been in a similar predicament at one time or another, when we just couldn't remember the name of a familiar acquaintance. It's a fact that most of us easily remember faces of people we've met only once or twice. The problem comes in attaching a name to that face, since most of us find it far easier to remember what we see than what we hear. In general, we remember names we often come across; those we seldom see require more organized effort to recall.

# What's Your Name Again?

There is probably nothing so important to a person as his or her own name. When you go into a store, a business, or a restaurant and are greeted by name, you are being given the indirect message that you matter. This is why forgetting someone's name can be particularly embarrassing and why people who always seem to remember everyone's name are highly regarded.

Michael and Sarah were shopping one afternoon when suddenly an old business acquaintance ran up to Michael and pumped his hand. "Michael! Wonderful to see you!"

Sarah watched politely as Michael smiled and shook hands, obviously recognizing the man but not introducing him to her. Standing beside him for several minutes, she began to feel awkward and was inwardly fuming at Michael for his social gaffe. Finally, she extended her hand politely to the man and introduced herself.

"Hi there. I'm Sarah Ferguson."

The man politely shook her hand and offered a greeting without giving his own name, and Michael's discomfort increased. It was not until the man departed that Michael admitted to Sarah he couldn't remember the man's name and therefore could not introduce him to her.

# Why Are Faces Easier to Remember Than Names?

The memory of a face activates a region in the right part of the brain that specializes in spatial configurations. But recent research has found that the brain systems that learn and remember faces are found in a completely different place from those that learn and recall other things, such as man-made objects. While the face memory is stored in the part of the brain responsible for spatial configurations, the memory of a blender, for example, activates areas that govern movement and touch. Scientists believe the difference in remembering these types of information lies in how the brain acquires knowledge. In other words, this theory holds that memories are stored in the same systems that originally recorded the information about the things being remembered. In the case of the blender, the memory is found in the part of the brain that originally processed how the blender felt and how the hands operated it. This leads scientists to suspect that names may be processed in a different part of the brain as well.

Another reason why we remember faces better than names is that the brain is involved in two separate processes—recognition and recall—and recognition is much easier for the brain to accomplish than recall. Recognition requires a person to choose among a limited number of alternatives, but remembering requires a far more complex mental process. The difference between recall and recognition can be explained in this way:

## Recall

Who was the president of the United States during the Civil War?

## Recognition

Who was president during the Civil War?

**(a)** Benjamin Franklin

**(b)** Abraham Lincoln

**(c)** John Quincy Adams

Finally, most people simply aren't attentive enough when they are introduced; and if you're not paying attention, you won't be able to recall the name later on.

## Why Do We Forget Names We Know Well?

But why do we sometimes forget the names of people we know very well—names that we have known for a long time? Scientists think one reason why this may happen is that memory for proper nouns appears to be different from memory for common nouns. But they don't know why this is so, or why memory for proper nouns is particularly susceptible to age and stress. Some researchers believe that our memory systems treat proper nouns more like the vocabulary of a foreign language than the words of our mother tongue.

If you're finding it hard to remember names, ask yourself these questions:

■ Did you pay attention when you first heard the name?

■ Did you rehearse the name enough to register it?

■ Were you tense or preoccupied as you heard the name?

■ Were you distracted while being introduced?

# Verbal Techniques for Remembering Names

When it comes to remembering names, there are two groups of mnemonics that may be helpful—verbal techniques and visual imagery methods. In this chapter, we'll discuss various techniques for remembering and associating names and faces.

By far the easiest is a simple verbal technique involving repeating and using the person's name out loud after an introduction. Try this method:

- Register the person's name—pay attention!

- Repeat the person's name to yourself.

- Comment on the name.

- Use the person's name, out loud, as soon as possible.

## Pay Attention When You Are Introduced

In most cases, you don't forget someone's name; you just never really heard it in the first place. Perhaps you were worrying about the impression you were making. Maybe you were looking over the person's shoulder thinking about the next people you would meet.

It should be no surprise that research has found that the more self-conscious you are, the more likely you will not be able to remember a person's name. This is because self-conscious people tend to pay an inordinate amount of attention to themselves in social situations: "Do I look all right? Does he like me? What should I say next?"

The first trick, then, to remembering a name is to be sure that you're paying attention when you first hear it. The next time you're introduced to a new person, pay attention. Don't think about yourself—concentrate fully on the other person, screening out every other person in the room. Really look at the person's face and listen intently to the new name.

If you don't quite hear the name or it is difficult to pronounce, immediately stop and ask the person who introduced you to repeat the name. You'd be surprised at the number of people who are reluctant to do this, fearing to appear inattentive or rude.

## Repeat the Name

"Sue, I'd like you to meet Joe Hanover." As Sue is staring at Joe, she should repeat his name to herself: "Joe Hanover. Joe Hanover." Then she should spell the name to herself. If she can't spell the name, she should ask the person how the name is spelled.

The reason that repeating and spelling the name to yourself is important is because these actions will help ensure you have paid attention to the name in the first place. It will also help impress the name on your memory.

## Comment on the Name

Because people tend to remember anything better if it is unusual, try to make some comment about the person's name. Obviously, this is easier if the name is at all foreign or uncommon.

Many times, on hearing my name for the first time people will ask: "Are you related to Fran, the football player?" No, I explain, it's *Turkington,* not *Tarkenton.* Literati wonder if I am related to Booth. No, I explain, it's *Turkington,* not *Tarkington.* Then there are those who wonder whether I'm related to Christy, the model. No, I say, it's *Turkington,* not *Turlington.*

# Use the Name in Conversation

Soon after being introduced, repeat the person's name in conversation. Take the first opportunity to reintroduce the person to another acquaintance so that you have a chance to use the first *and* last names soon after hearing them. You may feel self-conscious about repeating another's first name, but it's usually possible to get away with this several times in a conversation without attracting undue attention to yourself. You can repeat the name once after you've been introduced, insert it at least once during the conver-sation ("Do you agree, Betty?"), and then use it again when you say good-bye.

# Visual Techniques for Remembering Names

Since it seems clear that it's easier to remember visual than auditory information, one of the best ways to remember names is to make the information visual. Among the various memory strategies that use visual imagery, the face-name association method was designed specifically for learning names. To use this technique, after registering the person's name (remember—*pay attention!*):

- Associate the name with something meaningful.
- Note distinctive features of the person's face.
- Form a visual association between the name and the distinctive feature.

## Associate the Name with Something Meaningful

When you're trying to remember a person's name upon first meeting him or her, it helps to associate the last name with something concrete. That's not hard to do if the name is something like

Black, Taylor, Smith, or Bales. The problem comes when the name does not readily bring to mind anything meaningful—especially if the name sounds foreign.

For example, "Begleiter" does not bring to mind anything concrete, but it can be broken down into something that sounds meaningful—"big lighter." Some more examples:

Sokal—soak oil

Roulston—roll son

Flaherty—flayed heart

If you meet someone whose name is so unusual that you just can't translate it into anything meaningful, the effort you've put into trying to do so will help you remember the name.

# Look for Distinctive Facial Features

If you want to link a name and a face, it helps if you can make a vivid association between the two. It's likely that anyone meeting Beauty and the Beast wouldn't have trouble remembering them, because both would be equally memorable: faces that are quite beautiful or quite unattractive tend to stay in your mind. Studies also suggest that faces of your own race are easier to remember.

But it's not always easy to find something distinctive in a face, especially if you haven't been trained to do so. But it is possible to get better at this. It's likely that a city person confronted with a herd of cows will think they all look alike; but to the dairyman in charge of the animals, each is quite distinctive. It's the same way with faces. You don't think so?

Look at the hair. Is it:

- long or short?

- thick or thin?

- curly or straight?

- colorful or mousy?

- coarse or fine?

- attractively styled or sloppy?

Now check out the eyes. Are they:

- blue or brown, green or gray?

- narrow or wide?

- close together or far apart?

- popeyed or deep-set?

- long-lashed or short-lashed?

- reddened or clear?

- warm and affectionate, or cold and distant?

Is the nose:

- long or short?

- fat or thin?

- humped or straight?

- tilting up or curling down?

- flanked by wide, narrow, or flaring nostrils?

- pockmarked or fine-pored?

- reddened or flesh-toned?

Other characteristics to examine:

- Do the cheeks puff out?

- Is the forehead high and smooth or low and furrowed?

- Do the ears stick out like wing nuts, or are they fashioned close to the head?

- Does the chin recede or jut out? Is it cleft with a dimple or covered with little hairs?

Any or all of these characteristics, taken together, can make a person's face more memorable than you first realized. Of all the characteristics, research says, the hair is typically the most distinctive, but hairstyle and hair color are also easy to change. Whatever you have to work with, practice looking closely at a person's face to pick out one feature that is interesting.

## Make a Visual Association between the Name and the Feature

Once you've picked a distinctive feature, make a visual association between that feature and the name. Say you've just met Sam Stone, who has a high, broad forehead. Picture that smooth, white forehead in your eye; it's almost like marble, or stone. By linking the name "Stone" with the memorable feature of the marblelike forehead, you've made it easy to remember Sam's last name. The next time you want to remember a name, here's how to do it using the name-face association method:

- Pay attention to the name and repeat it.
- Think about the name and find something distinctive in it.
- Scrutinize the person's face; choose something memorable.
- Link the memorable feature with the distinctive name and picture it vividly in your mind.

## Make Pictures with Names

Unfortunately, not everyone has Jay Leno's distinctive chin or Bob Hope's memorable nose. For an even simpler method that does not require a distinctive face, try making a picture with the

Remember a name by making a mental picture of it.

person's name alone. Bill Smith could be visualized as a black-smith with a long, rounded nose like a duck's bill.

# Review the Associations

After you've done all you can to remember someone's name, it's important to review it as soon as possible after meeting someone, and then repeat it again to yourself in about fifteen seconds, and yet again a few minutes later. If you've met several people within a short space of time, practice reviewing them all at the end of the social event.

If you're meeting several people in a row—if you're the new employee in an office, for example—you can reduce the chance of confusing the names by meeting each person in a different setting, if possible. The more time that elapses between introductions, the better your chances of remembering the names.

Using the steps outlined above, it should be possible to remember what seems like an astonishing number of names. People who have been trained in these techniques report they can manage to remember very large groups of names—as many as several hundred if required.

# Remember Speeches and Foreign Languages

The worst thing you can do when faced with the task of giving a speech is to sit down and commit that speech to memory, word for word, on the assumption that you'll then be able to give the speech without notes.

In the first place, a memorized speech sounds like what it is—memorized speech. It lacks spontaneity and verve; even the best speaker tends to sound monotonous when blandly reciting a prewritten spiel. Moreover, if you've committed the speech to memory and you forget one word, you can get seriously flustered.

Some people avoid this problem by reading their speeches, but that's even worse—even if you manage to look up at your audience once in a while, there's nothing more deadly dull than someone standing up and reading words they've written down. And you risk losing your place and having to fumble through your papers to find where you left off.

The best choice is to be able to stand up in front of an audience and naturally, in your own words, simply have a conversation with the audience—talk about what you want to say. The very best speakers have mastered this technique, and you can, too. The thought of doing this throws most people without mnemonic training into catatonia, since fear of public speaking is one of the most common fears there is.

Fortunately, you can learn a variety of mnemonic devices to retain the contents of a speech or script for delivery or use whenever you want, without having to learn the whole thing word for word or reading any part of it. Since all speeches are really just thoughts strung together in sequence, the key is to deliver the speech using your own words and following the logical sequence.

To perform any speech in this way, first write out the entire text so that it includes the most important points and everything else you want to say. Read it over to get the feel of it. Now you're ready to apply the first of the mnemonics.

# Mnemonic Techniques for Speakers

## The Method of Loci

The oldest method of remembering speeches is the method of loci, which we discussed in chapter 4. This ancient mnemonic strategy involves mentally placing information in imaginary locations. To remember the items, you simply recall the locations.

To use this method to remember a speech, first envision a well-known place such as your home or a large public building you know well. You'll be visualizing a series of locations within this building, placing the parts of your speech around the different areas.

An easy way to do this is to start with the front door of your own home, enter the living room, and proceed from there to the dining room, the kitchen, and so on. For more clues to help recall information, you can subdivide the space in a particular room. For example, in the living room, you can visualize the sofa as one location, the mantel as another, and the chair as another.

You must hold these familiar locations clearly in your mind's eye, making sure you establish a set of locations that are always seen in the same order. To associate new information in the order in which it is to be remembered, you place the information in a particular location in the house. Here's how to use the system when you want to remember a speech:

1. Write out the main points of your speech.

2. Sketch the layout of your home.

3. Visualize the first point of your speech at your front door.

4. Visualize the second point in your entry hall, and so on.

5. When you're standing at the podium and you're ready to give your speech, simply open your front door, enter the hall, and mentally work your way around the rooms.

Sound difficult? It really isn't.

Here's how you could remember the Gettysburg Address, using this method:

■ First, visualize your front door with the words "four score and seven" scrawled like graffiti on the wood.

- Now, swing open the front door and step into the hall. Right in front of you is a staircase; visualize our forefathers crowded on the steps, dressed in top hats or Puritan garb.

- On the telephone table against the wall, picture a continent, balancing precariously, wearing a sash proclaiming "new nation" across its front.

- As you step into the living room, visualize the Statue of Liberty reclining on the sofa.

- On the mantel, picture a lady of the evening propositioning a patron.

- On the television, visualize a giant neon equal sign.

When it's time to remember the Gettysburg speech, open the door. When you visualize the staircase, you will remember the key word "forefathers." When the telephone table comes into view the words "continent" and "new nation" will spring to mind. In the living room, you'll remember "conceived in liberty," "proposition," and "equal."

# Link Systems

You can also memorize main points in a speech by choosing a key word to represent an entire thought, and then linking those key words. Let's take the Gettysburg Address again. Say you're President Lincoln, and you have a general idea of what you want to say—you just need a bit of a reminder of the sequence of your thoughts.

- The first key word is "new nation"; envision a baby wearing an Uncle Sam hat.

- Link that to the next key word, "civil war"—picture the baby in the Uncle Sam hat fighting with a civet.

To memorize the Gettysburg Address by using the method of loci,
start by visualizing your front door with the first words
of the Address written on it.

- Link the civet to "dedicate" (dead crate)—imagine the civet being put, dead, into a crate. Link that to "unfinished work" by perching the crate on top of an unfinished wok.

---

## The Gettysburg Address

*Four score and seven years ago, our fathers brought forth on this continent, a new nation, conceived in Liberty, and dedicated to the proposition that all men are created equal.*

*Now we are engaged in a great civil war, testing whether that nation, or any nation so conceived and so dedicated, can long endure. We are met on a great battle-field of that war. We have come to dedicate a portion of that field, as a final resting place for those who here gave their lives that that nation might live. It is altogether fitting and proper that we should do this.*

*But, in a larger sense, we can not dedicate—we can not consecrate—we can not hallow—this ground. The brave men, living and dead, who struggled here, have consecrated it, far above our poor power to add or detract. The world will little note, nor long remember what we say here, but it can never forget what they did here. It is for us the living, rather, to be dedicated here to the unfinished work which they who fought here have thus far so nobly advanced. It is rather for us to be here dedicated to the great task remaining before us—that from these honored dead we take increased devotion to that cause for which they gave the last full measure of devotion—that we here highly resolve that these dead shall not have died in vain—that this nation, under God, shall have a new birth of freedom—and that government of the people, by the people, for the people, shall not perish from the earth.*

# Foreign-Language Techniques

Whether you are trying to learn a new foreign language or retain one you learned years ago, it's vital that you practice both the passive stage of understanding (recognition) and the active stage of speaking and writing (recall).

## Experience the Language

In order to maintain memory for a language, you must experience the language in written or oral form. Otherwise, your active vocabulary will shrink, although your passive understanding will remain. Both recognition and recall, however, depend on proficiency, exposure, and practice. Try these strategies:

- Listen to the radio in the foreign language. Shortwave radios bring in broadcasts in many languages from around the world. Make a note of when the programs are aired, and try to be a consistent listener.

- Listen to language tapes designed to teach the language, or listen to taped books in the language.

- Read books or newspapers at least once a week in the language. Reading is one of the best ways to keep a language alive in your consciousness.

- Take continuing-education courses to brush up on grammar and speak the language aloud with others.

- Rent or go see movies in the language, and listen to the language while looking at the subtitles.

- Take advantage of opportunities to practice conversing in the language with a foreign-exchange student or a neighbor from a foreign country. Never miss a chance to speak the language, however briefly. The more contact you can retain with the language, the more easily it will come back to you.

Although it is harder to learn a foreign language later in life, the greater the previous knowledge of the language, the more mental references there will be to facilitate new learning.

# Use the Key-Word Mnemonic

One of the best ways to learn foreign language vocabulary is to use the key-word mnemonic, which utilizes a two-step approach. For example, the French word for hat is *chapeau*. In order to learn this word, transform *chapeau* into the key word *chap*. Next, form a visual image connecting this key word with the English meaning. You could picture a fierce wind that will surely chap your face unless you wear a hat.

To remember the meaning of the French word for father, *pere,* transform it into the key word *pear* and think of a giant pear with your father's face.

Here is a list of everyday French nouns together with possible key words:

A cat is a *chat* (shah); picture the shah of Iran shaking hands with a huge cat.

A nose is a *nez* (neigh); picture a horse with a huge nose, neighing.

A pair of eyeglasses are *lunettes* (loon-ettes); picture a loon wearing a pair of glasses.

A pair of socks are *chausettes* (show sets); you show a set of socks to a friend.

A tip is a *pourboire* (poor boy); you tip a poor boy.

Now test yourself.

*Chat* means _____.

*Nez* means _____.

*Lunettes* are _____.

*Chausettes* are _____.

*Pourboire* means _____.

*S    T    E    P*

# Remember
# Numbers

There's no doubt that remembering numbers is one of the most critical types of everyday remembering we have to do. The important numbers in our lives include phone numbers, street numbers, Social Security numbers, credit cards, license plates, ages, identification numbers, and prices. But because numbers are so abstract, remembering them can be one of the most difficult memory tasks.

Still, most people find there are a few numbers they have no trouble remembering. There's usually a reason for this. One woman, who has a terrible time remembering her own wedding anniversary, always remembers the birth date of her only child, because it is so visual—the child was born on January 23, or 1/23.

Another friend remembers his Social Security number because in college that number served as his "student number." He had to write it so many times, over and over, that it became imprinted permanently in his memory.

When encountering a number, a person's eyes first register the individual digits; once this visual sensory input enters the brain, the information is retained just long enough to be remembered briefly. Selected bits of this information may enter long-term memory if the numbers are rehearsed or repeated over and over, or if there is a strong sensory or emotional component to the number.

If motivation is high, or you have plenty of practice in remembering a certain type of number (prices in a grocery store or statistics connected with your job),, it can be easier to remember numbers. But when motivation is lacking or the number is just too long, remembering numbers can be made easier by using one of several memory strategies.

# Chunking

Chunking—breaking long numbers down into reasonable bits—is one of the easiest techniques for remembering numbers. For example, the number 8005552943 is difficult to remember, but when its digits are grouped into a telephone number style, the task becomes much easier. As a telephone number, the sequence becomes (800) 555-2943, a fairly simple number to maintain in short-term memory.

# Simple Visualization

Some people who find it very easy to visualize simply imagine the number they are trying to remember painted as bright purple graffiti against a white wall. The actual color and location of the number are not as important as the brightness and clarity of the vision; the more unusual, the better. Perhaps you could visualize the number as dripping with starlight against the black night sky, or encrusted with diamonds on a black velvet jewel case.

If possible, try to make a verbal association with the visual impression; comment out loud on your visualization. If you're trying to remember the dimensions of your living-room window—42 by 82—so you can buy the correct size blinds, visualize the window vividly with the numbers emblazoned on the glass while saying to yourself, "I'm hanging these blinds when I'm 42. I wonder if they'll still be here when I'm 82."

# Numerical Relationships

You can also remember a number by identifying relationships among its digits. For example, you can more easily remember the number 246-1369 by noticing that the first three numbers count forward by twos, and the second group of numbers count forward by threes. While not all important numbers will have any identifiable relationship, many do.

# Secret-Code Method

Another way to remember numbers is to create words out of them. There are many ways to do this; for example, to remember the number 543, give each number its alphabetical equivalent ($A$ = 1, $B$ = 2, and so on). The number 543 would translate into the letters *EDC*. Next, create a sentence with words beginning with those letters: "Eventually dawn comes." To remember the numbers, simply recall the sentence and transform its initial letters back into the numbers they represent.

# Phonetic Peg System

The peg system is a good way to remember numbers, although it is fairly complicated. As we learned in chapter 6, each number is translated into a corresponding letter or sound:

1 = *t* or *d*
2 = *n*
3 = *m*
4 = *r*
5 = *l*
6 = *sh* or *ch*
7 = *k,* hard *c,* or *g*
8 = *f, v,* or *ph*
9 = *p,* or *b*
0 = *z* or *s*

Once the list has been memorized thoroughly, so that you can automatically connect each number with its corresponding letter sound, you can apply this method to remembering long strings of numbers.

If you want to remember a seven-digit telephone number, you would first translate each numeral into its corresponding letter and then make a word (or words) out of the number, inserting vowels where necessary. Remembering the word will be the key to remembering the entire telephone number.

Try this method with the phone number 342-4350. The corresponding letters would become:

mrnrmls

After adding vowels, the phrase becomes:

MR. NoRMaLS

The list of numbers and corresponding letters must be memorized perfectly for this method to work well.

# Picture Code

The visual peg system can also be used to remember numbers. As we learned in chapter 6, each number is matched to a letter that resembles the number:

1 = spear
2 = swan
3 = pitchfork
4 = sailboat
5 = spread-out hand
6 = snake
7 = gallows
8 = hourglass
9 = snail
0 = plate

With this system, each number is represented by an obvious symbol (0 looks like a dinner plate, 2 resembles a swan, and so forth). To remember the airline flight number 3678, simply visualize a pitchfork threatening a snake inching towards a gallows while an hourglass marks the time until the execution.

# Aerobic Exercise

If you're still having problems remembering numbers, you might consider some more unorthodox methods. Some researchers believe that short-term memory for numbers can be improved through aerobic exercise. While researchers aren't sure why this is true, they suspect it may be linked to an increase in oxygen efficiency or a rise in glucose metabolism in the brain. Good examples of aerobic exercise include brisk walking, cycling, swimming, jogging, and racquet sports. The exercise should be done at least three times weekly for thirty minutes at a time.

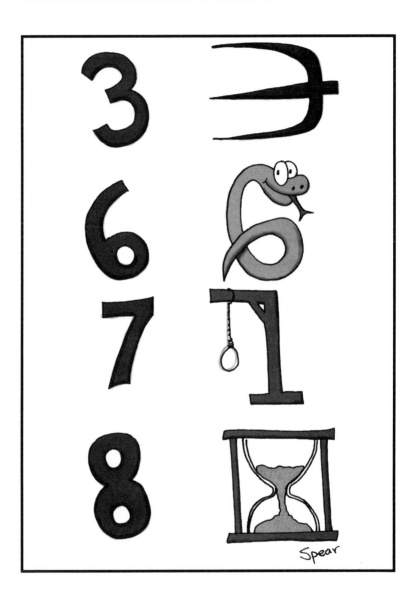

A good way to remember numbers is to use the picture code.

# Twelve-Digit Code for Dates

To figure out any date in the year, all you need to learn is a simple twelve-digit code representing the first Sunday in each of the twelve months. For 1995, the code is 155-274-263-153. This means that the first Sunday in January is January 1, the first Sunday in February is February 5, the first Sunday in July is July 2, and so on.

To find the day of the week for August 3, note that the first Sunday in August is August 6, and count back three days to find that August 3 is a Thursday. Here's a harder one: to find the day of the week for October 30, note that the first Sunday in the month is October 1. Add seven to get the second Sunday (October 8), and add three more sevens to get to the fifth Sunday (October 29). Count forward one day to arrive at October 30, which falls on a Monday.

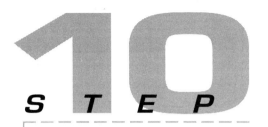

# Improve Your Study Methods

**D**avid doesn't like history, but he grudgingly sat down and read over the entire chapter before the week's exam. But when he sat down to take the test, the entire experience of studying medieval history vanished from his memory.

What was going on?

First, David's resentment probably interfered with his concentration, since attitude is an important component of attention. Unmotivated, the memory simply does not do a very good job of retaining information. But the way David went about his reading assignment was also part of the problem.

He simply read the chapter from beginning to end, without questioning, commenting, or categorizing. He just sat down and opened the book with a vague hope that he would remember what he was reading. That's rather like throwing a batch of file cards into a drawer and hoping you'll be able to pick out what you'll need later on.

Problems like David's are not unusual. In tests of students who participated in studies of nondirected reading, retention rates a day later were only about 20 percent.

It doesn't have to be that way.

After those same students learned some fairly simple strategies (discussed in this chapter), retention rates increased to more than 80 percent. Research over the past twenty years has shown that mnemonics can help improve memory for schoolwork, including spelling, vocabulary words, foreign-language vocabulary (including abstract and concrete nouns and verbs), names and accomplishments of historical figures, states and capitals, specialized scientific terms, reading, cities and their primary products, U.S. presidents, foreign kings, basic mathematics, and more.

Yet for many years the idea of "mnemonics" has been unpopular in educational circles. Many educators have been reluctant to embrace the techniques, despite the fact that research has shown that they can help both poor and good students as young as fourth graders remember important information. Studies suggest that gifted students may benefit most of all.

Why this reluctance despite the evidence? One of the most common objections has been that mnemonics are not relevant to school subjects because they don't help students understand what they learn. There also seems to be a basic psychological mistrust of mnemonics as "trickery," as if the material remembered using mnemonics is somehow less valid than material learned in other ways.

Proponents of mnemonic techniques counter that, since most schoolwork involves rote memorization, it makes sense to memorize tasks more efficiently. This frees students to spend more time in creative analysis and other advanced educational tasks.

# Techniques for Recording Information

These tips will help you record information efficiently so that you will be more likely to remember it later on.

## Involve Yourself in Your Reading

If you have trouble retaining written material, here are a few suggestions to help you get actively involved in your reading:

- Come up with questions for yourself before, during, and after the reading session.

- Ask yourself what is happening in the text, why it's happening, and what would happen if one event or fact was different.

- Note what interests you. Take a moment to make some mental comments, out loud if possible.

- Train yourself to summarize, a section at a time. What are the main points in the text you just read? What are the logical conclusions and ramifications?

## Visualize as You Read

As you read, try to imagine yourself in the place you're reading about, or try to imagine yourself actually doing what you are studying. Include yourself in images that you construct in your mind. If you're reading about the Civil War, picture yourself on the battlefield. Why are you there? What is the enemy doing, and why? The better you are able to put yourself into the scene, the better you will remember what you are reading. When it comes time to take the test, the other students will have read the material, but *you* will have been there!

Of course, it's a lot easier to remember yourself experiencing historical events than it is to link yourself to the major exports of Argentina. Instead of just trying to memorize "beef, wool, and wheat," imagine that you are an Argentinean farmer raising cattle and sheep and growing crops to make a living.

This will work with any subject except those involving numbers, dates, and similar material.

## Take Good Notes as You Listen

Does taking notes help you remember? That all depends on how you take them. Do you take copious notes as if by rote, scribbling down word for word without thinking about the content of the message? Unfortunately, that's the way far too many students take notes. Most people simply try to write down everything their teacher says and fail to listen carefully. When you review your notes later, it's hard to interpret them.

The best way to take notes is to take them carefully while thinking about their content. Review them several times as you write, and summarize whenever possible. Isolate what's important, and discard the rest while you're writing.

# The PQRST Method

One of the most popular memory techniques used as a study method is the PQRST technique, which is helpful when trying to remember facts. This acronym stands for Preview, Question, Read, State, and Test. Memory experts believe this method works better than simple rehearsal because it provides better retrieval cues. It also may work because it closely parallels your situation during original learning.

# Preview

Skim through the material briefly. Read the preface, table of contents, and chapter summaries. Preview a chapter by studying the outline and skimming the chapter (especially headings, photos, graphs, or charts). The object here is to get an overview of what the book or chapter is all about; this shouldn't take more than a few minutes. Most chapters in textbooks have a summary at the end of the chapter; be sure to read the summary first, before you read the chapter. This will help you be prepared to recognize the main points. Completing this overview will give you a good general idea of the content of the material.

To fully understand how a good preview can help you organize and understand information, try reading the following paragraph, which appeared in *Your Memory* by Kenneth Higbee:

> *The procedure is really quite simple. First you arrange things into different groups. Of course, one pile may be sufficient depending on how much there is to do. If you have to go somewhere else due to lack of facilities, that is the next step; otherwise you are pretty well set. It is important not to overdo things. That is, it is better to do too few things at once than too many. After the procedure is completed, arrange the materials into different groups again. They can then be put into their appropriate places. Eventually they will be used once more and the whole cycle will then have to be repeated.*

Difficult to understand? Now go back and read the paragraph again with the knowledge that it is a description of how to do laundry. When you understand the context of the description, suddenly the entire passage makes far more sense.

## Question

Ask important questions about the information you're reading. "What are the primary points in the text? How does the action occur? Who is involved?" Read over the paragraph headings and ask yourself questions about them. If the chapter includes review questions at the end of the chapter, read them *before* you begin reading the chapter itself.

## Read

Now read the material completely, without taking notes. Underlining text can help you remember the information, provided you do it correctly. The first time you read a chapter, do not underline anything. It's very difficult to pick out the main points on the first reading. As with taking notes in class, many people tend to underline far too much.

Instead, read one section without underlining; then go back and, as you work your way through each paragraph, underline the important points. Think about the points you are underlining and whether they are truly the most important ones.

## State

Next, state the answers out loud to key questions. Reread the chapter and ask yourself questions; answer them out loud. Read what you've underlined out loud and think about what you're saying. You should spend about half of your studying time stating information out loud.

## Test

Test yourself to ensure that you have retained the information. Go through the chapter again, asking yourself questions. Space out your testing so that you're doing it during a study session, after a study session, and right before a test. Testing yourself right before an exam is not the same thing as "cramming." Cramming implies that you have never before seen the material and you are madly trying to learn it before the exam. Testing yourself is simply an effective method of reviewing the information before the exam.

# Make the Most of Your Study Time

When it comes to studying properly, timing is everything. If you've got a big test coming up, it's better to schedule several shorter study sessions instead of one marathon all-night session. You should also use different methods while you're learning information: take notes one day, make an outline the next, recite information out loud at another time, and discuss the material with someone else at still another session.

## Avoid Interference

Susan and Joe were both studying for an economics final. After Susan closed her economics textbook, she read the evening paper, flipped through a fashion magazine, and then watched a TV show before picking up her French book for another hour of studying before bedtime. Joe, on the other hand, simply studied for his economics final and then went to bed. When the two reviewed the material just before the economics final, Joe had a much better grasp of it, because he had not allowed anything else to interfere with the information he had studied. Research has also shown that sleeping between studying and testing is the best way to do well on a test, since a person who sleeps right after studying will remember more than someone who stays awake.

It's also true that other activities between studying and taking a test can have a big effect on how well you remember the information. For example, if you've spent several hours studying German, you should not study another foreign language before going to bed, because the similarity of the information will interfere with distinguishing the information proper to each.

In fact, if you have two very similar subjects to study, it's best not to study them in the same location, for that will also tend to cause interference. Studying French in your bedroom and Spanish in the dining room or anthropology in the kitchen and sociology in the den will help you keep the two separate when you recall them.

## Space Your Study Sessions

It's far better to spend three separate one-hour sessions studying German than it is to study three hours at one time. One study that tested this theory found that groups who followed these alternative study schedules initially achieved similar results, but the group that spaced out its studying retained the information better four days later.

Spacing out your study sessions probably works because you can concentrate only for a certain period of time. If you try to do all your studying at one time, you will not be able to maintain concentration. Research also shows that breaks help you consolidate what you've learned, especially if you review the material in your mind during the breaks.

Of course, there is a limit to how much you can break down your study sessions. Scheduling too many short study sessions is actually worse than cramming all the studying into one marathon session. The trick, then, is to determine the optimum length of a study session and how many sessions work best. Research suggests that difficult information, inexperienced students, and early stages of learning require shorter study sessions for best results.

Similarly, if you have several subjects to study, it's better to study the subjects in separate sessions than all at once. It's best if you can space out the study sessions over several days.

# Use Peg Systems in Your Studies

It's possible to use the peg word method (as described in chapter 6) for a variety of scholastic tasks. This method is especially useful if you have a long list of information to be memorized. For example, if you needed to learn the hardness of minerals, you could substitute a word for each mineral—*pie* for pyrite, for example—and then associate it with the appropriate peg word. Since pyrite is of hardness six, you could envision a pie with sticks sticking out of it like candles.

The peg system is helpful when you must learn a list of items whose numerical order is important, such as the Bill of Rights:

1 = bun (hot cross bun) (freedom of religion)

2 = shoe (shoo-ting) (freedom to bear arms)

3 = tree (soldiers using a tree trunk to batter down your door to take over your house) (no soldiers quartered in homes)

4 = door (soldiers opening your door to search your house) (freedom from unjustified search and seizure)

5 = hive (defendant sitting on a hive, "taking the fifth") (legal rights)

6 = sticks (judge prodding lawyers to put you on trial) (right to a speedy trial)

7 = heaven (twelve jurors stacked up to heaven) (right to a jury trial)

8 = gate (person being hanged from a gate) (no cruel and unusual punishment)

9 = vine (wicked witch crawling up a vine shouting, "I have my rights!") (individual retention of rights not outlined in Constitution)

10 = hen (fifty states crammed into a henhouse fighting over their rights) (states' rights)

Others have used the peg system to learn the names of the U.S. presidents, lists of names, recipe ingredients, and reasons why dinosaurs became extinct. One study found it's even possible to use the peg system to learn the steps in a task, such as how to change the printwheel on a printer.

# Try Link Systems to Learn

The link system can be used in many school situations that require rote memorization of lists. If you have to learn the U.S. presidents in order, you could try the link method. To remember the first five presidents:

George Washington
John Adams
Thomas Jefferson
James Madison
James Monroe

- Picture George Washington hanging out the wash at the *dam* (Adams).

- The dam is holding back a lake of *java* (Jefferson).

- Java spills on the table, where the *mat's on* (Madison).

- The mat's on fire, so the *man rows* (Monroe) out to put it out.

You can use the key-word mnemonic to learn the capital of each state when someone tells you the state, or the vice president when someone gives you the president.

| *State* | *Capital* |
| --- | --- |
| Pennsylvania (Penn) | Harrisburg (harassing) |

Visualize William Penn harassing the Indians.

Learn the presidents in order by using the link method. Picture George Washington hanging out the wash at the <u>dam</u> (Adams).

To recall the state and the capital, use the link method to link the states together and the key-word mnemonic to remember the capital of each state.

You can use the link method with other things to be learned in order, too, such as the fifty states in alphabetical order.

| | | |
|---|---|---|
| 1. Alabama | 18. Louisiana | 35. Ohio |
| 2. Alaska | 19. Maine | 36. Oklahoma |
| 3. Arizona | 20. Maryland | 37. Oregon |
| 4. Arkansas | 21. Massachusetts | 38. Pennsylvania |
| 5. California | 22. Michigan | 39. Rhode Island |
| 6. Colorado | 23. Minnesota | 40. South Carolina |
| 7. Connecticut | 24. Mississippi | 41. South Dakota |
| 8. Delaware | 25. Missouri | 42. Tennessee |
| 9. Florida | 26. Montana | 43. Texas |
| 10. Georgia | 27. Nebraska | 44. Utah |
| 11. Hawaii | 28. Nevada | 45. Vermont |
| 12. Idaho | 29. New Hampshire | 46. Virginia |
| 13. Illinois | 30. New Jersey | 47. Washington |
| 14. Indiana | 31. New Mexico | 48. West Virginia |
| 15. Iowa | 32. New York | 49. Wisconsin |
| 16. Kansas | 33. North Carolina | 50. Wyoming |
| 17. Kentucky | 34. North Dakota | |

To remember the states using the link method, start off with the first state in the alphabetical list—Alabama—and think of a substitute word that sounds like Alabama—something like *album*. Next, think of a substitute for the second state on the list—*baked Alaska*. Now try to associate *album* with *baked Alaska*—think of an album filled with pictures of baked Alaskas in all different colors.

Let's move on to the third state on the list, Arizona, with a sub-stitute term like *scary zone*. Picture a whole fleet of baked Alaskas careening through the sky to spooky music as they fly through the scary zone. Now comes the fourth state on the list, Arkansas—try the substitute word *ark*. Think of the scary zone becoming transformed into a Biblical land as the ark floats into view. This brings us to the fifth state, California—*calling horn*. Imagine the ark using its calling horn to greet anyone left alive after the flood.

California to Colorado (color a doe)—see the horn painting colors on a doe. Colorado to Connecticut (connected cats)—see the doe playing with a line of connected cats. Connecticut to Delaware (Della wears)—see the connected cats hanging over Della—she's wearing connected cats!

Delaware to Florida (flower)—see Della wearing flowers. Florida to Georgia (gorge)—see flowers growing all over a gorge. Georgia to Hawaii (haw-hee)—see a gorge filled with laughter—haw-hees. Hawaii to Idaho (Ida hoes)—see haw-hees echoing as Ida hoes.

Idaho to Illinois (annoy)—see Ida hoeing, annoyed. Illinois to Indiana (Indian)—see annoyed Indians on the rampage. Indiana to Iowa (I owe ya)—see Indians admitting "I owe ya" one. Iowa to Kansas (cans)—I owe ya a can. Kansas to Kentucky (can't tuck it)—cans exclaiming "I can't tuck it in!"

Here are some suggested substitute words for the rest of the states:

> Louisiana—losing Anna
>
> Maine—main
>
> Maryland—merry land
>
> Massachusetts—masses of socks
>
> Michigan—itchy man
>
> Minnesota—mini soda
>
> Mississippi—missing Pippi

Missouri—sore eye

Montana—mountain

Nebraska—grass

Nevada—nervy ida

New Hampshire—new hamster

New Jersey—new jersey

New Mexico—new masks

New York—new yolk

North Carolina—Carol

North Dakota—decoder

Ohio—hi-ho!

Oklahoma—old home

Oregon—ore's gone

Pennsylvania—Penn's vane

Rhode Island—rode

South Carolina—carry Ina south

South Dakota—sow's decoder

Tennessee—tennis shoes

Texas—taxes

Utah—yodel

Vermont—varmint

Virginia—beer and gin

Washington—washing's done

West Virginia—best virgin

Wisconsin—wise cousin

Wyoming—roaming

There are other ways to use substitute words with the names of the states. Instead of relying on similar sounds, you could think of pictures in connection with the states, such as igloos in Alaska, beaches in California, Disney World in Florida, leis in Hawaii, etc. The most important point is that the substitute words should have meaning for you, not necessarily for anyone else. This is why it's a good idea to make up your own substitute words.

# Experiment with the Method of Loci

You can use the method of loci to remember long lists of things. For example, here's how to memorize the Bill of Rights using the loci method:

1. freedom of religion
2. freedom to bear arms
3. no soldiers quartered in your house
4. unreasonable search and seizure
5. legal rights (including not testifying against oneself)
6. right to a speedy trial
7. trial by jury
8. prohibition of cruel and unusual punishment
9. people retain their rights
10. states retain most rights

■ As you approach your house, envision a cross (or star of David, etc.) on the front door (the first location).

■ Opening the door, you see a gun standing at attention in the hall (second location).

■ Going into the living room, you see a soldier sleeping on the couch (third location).

■ As you enter the dining room (fourth location), a soldier jumps up from the dining room table and tries to search you.

- Going into the kitchen (fifth location), you see a defendant refusing to testify at your kitchen table.

- Moving up the back stairs (sixth location), a judge runs by holding the scales of justice.

- In the upstairs hall (seventh location), you see twelve members of a jury stacked up against the walls.

- Turning into the right bedroom (eighth location), you see a prisoner hanging over the bed.

- Going into the middle bedroom (ninth location), you see a wicked witch shouting, "I know my rights! I know the law!"

- In the bathroom (tenth location), pictures of all fifty states are crowded around the fixtures, arguing about which state has the rights to wash its hands next.

# Maintain Memory with Age

Researchers once thought that around the age of thirteen a person's brainpower began a slow downward spiral that continued until, by the age of seventy or eighty, there would be barely enough brain wattage left to power a penlight.

It's just not so.

In fact, your memory does not automatically self-destruct as you age. There is some leeway over when and how much memory ability is lost, says gerontologist Robert Butler, M.D., winner of the Pulitzer Prize for his book *Why Survive? Being Old In America.* "There is no overall decline with age," Butler says. "In fact, judgment, memory accuracy, and general knowledge may increase."

# How Memory Ages

While some specific parts of memory may decline with age, overall memory remains strong at least through the 70s. Research studies have shown that the average 70-year-old performs as well on many memory tests as 30 percent of 20-year-olds. And many older folks in their 60s and 70s score significantly better in verbal intelligence than young people. Even better, it's possible to improve memory with age. Studies of nursing-home populations showed that patients were able to make significant improvements in memory through the use of rewards and cognitive challenges.

Interestingly, researchers have discovered that older people best remember things and events that occurred from the ages of 25 to 40 rather than after age 50. This is probably because most of a person's life goals were defined and struggled for during those years: jobs, relationship, marriage, and children. It's not that life gets dull in middle age, but it has become routine—and the brain is far better at remembering how you felt on your wedding day than what you were thinking about during your bridge game last Tuesday.

## Flashbulb Memories

This ability to remember momentous events is related to the "flash-bulb memory" phenomenon, in which an extremely emotional event is remembered clearly years later. For example, everyone remembers what he or she was doing when President Kennedy was shot, although not much is remembered about the day before or after. Part of the reason why momentous events are imprinted so strongly in the brain is that it's more than likely a person was paying attention when they occurred. Some experts also believe the burst of brain chemicals produced during times of great emotion or stress influences the formation of permanent memories, and almost certainly results in a memory that is encoded in a different way from everyday memories.

# The Decline of Memory

As a person ages, memory function begins to slow down, affecting different types of memory in different ways. Many of the reasons for this age-related memory loss are reversible—depression, medications (especially benzodiazepines used to treat anxiety), poor diet, thyroid deficiency, or substance abuse. Treating these problems or switching medications may completely alleviate the memory problem. Memory loss may also be caused a range of organic problems in the brain itself. Researchers have come up with several possible reasons for the overall phenomenon of age-related memory deterioration, although none has been conclusively proven.

Still, the inevitable memory loss that does occur with age is usually very slight. "One may not learn or remember quite as rapidly during healthy late life, but one may learn and remember nearly as well," says Dennis Selkoe, M.D., co-director of the Center for Neurologic Diseases at Brigham and Women's Hospital in Boston.

After about age 30, most people reach a plateau that is usually maintained until about age 60, explains psychologist K. Warner Schaie, Ph.D., director of the Gerontology Center at Pennsylvania State University. "After that, there are small declines depending on ability and sex. But it's not until the 80s that any sort of serious mental slowdown occurs." Dr. Schaie, who's been tracing the mental meanderings of 4,000 people for more than 30 years, is an international authority on mental stimulation and the aging brain.

Indeed, semantic memory (general vocabulary and knowledge about the world) often stays sharp through the 70s, but memory for names (especially those not used frequently) begins to decline after age 35. This type of slowed thinking may be especially apparent when dealing with new problems or a problem requiring immediate attention.

While short-term memory does not decline as a person ages, long-term and episodic memory (remembering the time and place something occurred) does deteriorate. Spatial visualization skills (the ability to recognize faces and find one's car) have already begun to wane in the 20s.

Age-related memory problems may also be caused by differences in techniques for storing information. Those people with the best ability to remember at any age tend to cloak new information with details, images, and "cues." When they are introduced to a new acquaintance, for example, they notice the physical appearance of the person and link it in some way to the person's name, fitting the introduction into a context they already understand.

As a person ages, it's harder to organize this information effectively. In fact, researchers have documented a drop in effective encoding strategies during the 20s and traced a further, more gradual decrease over the remainder of the human life span.

For these reasons, older people have the most problems when attempting unfamiliar tasks that require rapid processing—such as learning how to program a videocassette recorder or operate a computer.

Many older people find they have trouble paying attention and ignoring distractions in the environment, and they find they need longer learning time, especially when confronting new information. Older people also tend not to make as much use of associations and visual cues as younger people, even though they may have greater need of these cues.

# The Good News

The capacity to focus on a task or follow an argument remains strong throughout life. Also, immediate (or short-term) memory remains strong. In addition, most healthy older people have no problem recalling world knowledge (or semantic memory), such as the name of the president, children's birthdays, or how to drive to the bank. In fact, studies have shown that world knowledge is likely to increase with age.

Once information has been well learned, older folks don't forget it any faster than younger people. And while they may take longer to come up with information, the search technique they employ does not change with age. Searching occurs automatically, as well as consciously. The bad news, according to some neuropsychologists, is that memory may decline by 50 percent between ages 25 and 75—but the good news is that wisdom does not.

# Organic Memory Problems

There are also a wide range of organic reasons underlying memory loss in older people. As humans age, there appears to be a major loss of brain cells in the hippocampus and in other parts of the brain that control memory and learning. The death of these cells causes a drop in the production of neurotransmitters vital to memory and learning. Unfortunately, the hippocampus, one of the most important brain structures involved in memory, is also highly vulnerable to aging. Studies have found that up to 5 percent of the nerve cells in the hippocampus evaporate with each decade past middle age. This could mean a loss of up to 20 percent of total hippocampal nerve cells by the time a person enters his 80s. Damage to this area of the brain may be a result of stress hormones. Excessive amounts of free radicals (toxic forms of oxygen) can also build up as a person ages, damaging the hippocampus.

The speed with which we process information also decreases with age, so that it takes longer to retrieve stored material as the brain shrinks and the cells become less efficient.

Of course, things can happen to the brain to accelerate its decline. A person can be genetically unlucky, be exposed to toxins like lead or pesticides, or smoke and drink excessively. Many other conditions can also bring about memory problems if they aren't treated, including high blood pressure, diabetes, thyroid disorders, sight and hearing problems, and brain tumors.

No discussion of memory and the elderly would be complete without a brief look at senility, aging, and Alzheimer's disease. About half of elderly men and women with severe memory impairment have Alzheimer's disease, another fourth suffer from vascular disorders (such as stroke), and the rest have a variety of problems, including tumors, abnormal thyroid function, infections, adverse drug reactions, and abnormalities in the spinal fluid. A good diagnosis is important, since all these problems except for Alzheimer's can be treated.

Tests for progressive memory loss should include complete and thorough physical, psychiatric, and neurologic exams. This may include a detailed medical history, especially of certain hereditary disorders, exposure to toxic substances, and past injuries such as head injuries or ministrokes that may account for current memory problems.

Your doctor may order lab tests, including blood, sputum, and urine studies to check for imbalances of hormones or chemicals, toxic levels of medications, and infections.

An x-ray or CAT scan of the brain can help detect an infection, tumor, head injury, or structural abnormalities. Electroencephalograms  measure the electrical activity of the brain and can help detect brain tumors, infection, stroke damage, or other brain problems that could be causing a memory problem.

Finally, psychological tests and mental status exams are used to test memory and mental awareness and rule out emotional disorders.

# Is It Alzheimer's or Simple Forgetfulness?

How do you tell the difference between normal breakdown of memory with age (age-associated memory impairment, or AAMI) and Alzheimer's disease? While both begin with forgetfulness, Alzheimer's soon progresses to a far more profound memory loss than simply misplacing keys or forgetting a name.

If a patient misplaces his glasses, that's forgetfulness. If he can't remember that he *wears* glasses, that could be a sign of Alzheimer's. AAMI does not progress rapidly and may leave memory unchanged for years, whereas Alzheimer's disease is progressive, interfering more and more severely with the normal activities of daily life. Alzheimer's also affects more than memory— it interferes with the ability to use words, compute figures, solve problems, and use reasoning and judgment. It may also result in mood and personality changes.

The patient with Alzheimer's disease usually first has problems with short-term memory, forgetting recent events. The patient may neglect to turn off the oven, recheck to see if jobs are done, or repeat questions. As the disease worsens, the signs become more pronounced. The patient's conversation becomes more senseless, and judgment begins to be affected. The patient may wander from home and be unable to find the way back. Some patients even get lost inside their own homes.

Here's a test you can give yourself. Write down three common words: *chair, banana,* and *dog.* Study them as long as you think you need to, and then set a timer to ring five minutes later. Do something else during these five minutes—read a book, or apply your makeup. During this time, don't repeat those three words. When the timer rings, try to remember them.

People with Alzheimer's disease can't remember the words. If you miss one or two, retake the test later. If you've improved your score, you can relax. Patients with any sort of degenerative brain disease can't improve their score by retesting.

However, even if you fail this test several times, it still may not mean you have a serious disease. Your memory problems could be related to something else, such as depression.

## Memory and Depression

Depression is a very common problem in the United States. As many as one-fourth of all older Americans suffer from the disorder severely enough to warrant treatment. It's important to include depression in a discussion of memory and the elderly, because in older folks, depression may mimic senility, causing memory loss, confusion, disorientation, and inattention to personal needs.

This type of depression that can appear in the elderly is called *depressive pseudodementia,* and it is typically found in about 15 percent of all depressed older people. The good news is that, when it is properly treated, the memory problems and confusion caused by this type of depression disappear.

There are a number of differences between depression and true senility. In depression, symptoms appear suddenly, and patients can describe their memory problems in great detail. Senile people experience symptoms very slowly, and they may not even be aware of a problem. They cannot describe symptoms very well and often deny problems with memory.

Depressed patients aren't very motivated to participate in performance tests, but they actually perform better than they think they can. Senile people try hard to complete the tests and think they performed better than they really did. Unlike senile patients, depressed people can pay attention to a task and have no problems concentrating. They can answer most questions of general knowledge, such as their age, date, and address. They can cook, dress, do household chores, and find their way home. Senile patients are unable to perform these activities of daily living.

But let's say that you don't have an organic disease and you're not suffering from depression. You may notice that your memory does seem a little bit slower. So what can you do about it?

# How to Improve Your Memory

While it's true that a person's memory can become less effective with age, memory loss is generally the result of disuse rather than disease. The important thing is to determine what is causing the memory problem, and then deal with it. To counteract the problem in paying attention that is common among elderly people, you could develop what is called "selective attention through observation." Identify situations in which you have memory problems, and then define what you want to remember, why, and for how long.

If your mental organization is decaying, you can learn specific recall strategies. And just as it's possible to strengthen a muscle by lifting weights, it's also possible to challenge the brain to become more efficient.

"The use-it-or-lose it principle applies not only to maintaining muscular flexibility, but to memory as well," Dr. Schaie says. By running through some daily mental drills—sort of like practicing scales on a piano—a person can prevent intellectual breakdown. In fact, Dr. Schaie has discovered that you can reverse a downward mental slide through a combination of mental gymnastics and problem-solving skills. Physical exercise, too, when combined with mental stimulation, can play a role in improving memory function.

# Stimulate Your Memory

Stimulating the brain can stop brain cells from shrinking with age; it can even lead to an increase in brain size, resulting in memory improvements. Animal studies in California have shown that rats living stimulating lives, with plenty of toys in their cages, have larger outer brain layers with larger, healthier cells. Rats kept in a barren cage with nothing to play with were listless and had smaller brains.

Some scientists now believe that humans can achieve the same result, improving their memory function (and even reversing a decline) by challenging themselves with active learning or by living in an "enriched" environment, alive with colors, sounds, sights, smells.

Not only that: research found that exercised brain cells have more dendrites (the branchlike projections that allow the cells to communicate with each other). With age, a stimulating environment encourages the growth of these dendrites, and a dull environment lowers their number. Researchers conclude that fewer, smaller brain cells is the price a person pays for failing to stimulate the brain.

That's why scientists believe a person's socioeconomic status often predicts memory problems and mental decline, since people who don't have a lot of disposable income often can't afford very stimulating environments.

## Liven Up Your Surroundings

The first step in bolstering your memory is to improve the health of your brain cells by making your surroundings stimulating—and the more stimulating the better. Here's how:

- The easiest way to liven up a room is through the use of color: Paint the walls a bright shade, add colorful curtains and pictures.

- A fish tank can provide soothing noise and a relaxing, constantly changing area of interest. Research has shown that simply sitting in a chair and watching fish can lower blood pressure.

- Fill the room with books, make sure there is music playing, and have videotapes available.

- Set up a chessboard—and play an occasional game.

- Put out lots of family keepsakes, heirlooms, and photos—even souvenirs from past vacations—and change them every week.

- Erect a bird feeder or birdhouses outside your window. Keep a pair of binoculars and a paperback bird identification book handy, and keep a "bird diary" to log each species sighted.

- Try jigsaw puzzles (the more complicated, the better) and three-dimensional interlocking puzzles.

- Equip your room with a shortwave radio that can pick up international broadcasts, opening a window on the world.

## Develop a Positive Attitude

Stimulation is not just about your physical environment, however. It's also about *attitude:*

- Work on maintaining a positive attitude, and try to stay flexible—don't get locked into a routine, refusing to deviate. Develop a willingness to explore new areas; get out and about and involved with life.

- Any kind of educational or recreational activity that requires problem-solving is useful. What's not useful are passive or mindless activities. TV is okay if it is a program where you can guess what the contestants will do.

"Jeopardy" scores a hit in the brain-building department; "The Flintstones" doesn't.

- Take a course. Not so hot at math or science? Try art history, flower arranging, photography, or cooking.

- Teach a skill. If you have some type of specialized skill (business, painting, writing, nutrition), try teaching a course at a YMCA or YWCA, senior center, community college, or "open" or "free" college connected with a large university.

- Take an adventurous vacation. It doesn't have to be white-water rafting or mountain climbing. If you're not quite that adventurous, try an archeological expedition not too far from home. For an exotic change, how about a dolphin communication experiment in Hawaii? Seek information at travel agencies specializing in adventure tours or senior activities.

- If you have extra time, volunteer. Check out the local volunteer service bureau, hospitals, nursing homes, service organizations, elementary or high schools, and day care centers.

- For the ultimate mind challenge, get a computer. At the flip of a switch there is an almost limitless number of games, programs, and types of information available. Go to the local computer store for a tryout—computers are much more user-friendly than they used to be—or visit a younger relative and ask for a demonstration. By their very nature, computer games improve eye-hand coordination, attention skills, and memory in such fun ways it's not like learning at all. For a small extra fee, you can buy a modem to hook up to various computer networks that communicate over the telephone line. This is a great idea for those who are not so mobile, but whose minds are sharp. For the cost of a telephone call and a small monthly membership fee, a network provides instant access to a host of information: financial tips, consumer reports, libraries, encyclopedias, banks, universities, news, cooking columns, free coupon offers, shopping networks, sports scores, and more. Special-interest "bulletin boards" (often free) allow members to receive and send messages to other members and can build up strong networks of friends among people of all ages around the country. If you can't afford a computer, see if the local senior center or school has one for use by the community. Explore renting and leasing options, or buy a used machine. Often, computer buffs who outgrow a perfectly good machine and move on to a more sophisticated model are willing to let their old unit go for a song.

■ Join a group. Get involved with the community. Try politics, social clubs, service organizations, church or meditation groups, or animal protection leagues.

■ Find a new talent. Work on carving, piano lessons, or soapmaking. What about a ham radio license—you'll profit from learning the Morse code necessary for the license, and a license will open up communication with other radio operators around the world.

■ Learn American Sign Language. The visual language of the deaf community is great for developing eye-hand coordination, and the rigors of becoming fluent in ASL will quicken your mental reflexes. You can parlay this new skill into volunteering in the deaf community. (Don't expect to be able to learn enough ASL to function as a translator in a few months, however. ASL is a complex language and takes years to master. Still, many people find it fun to learn and a beautiful alternative means of expression.)

■ Take a basic automotive-care course. Offered at community colleges or technical schools (and sometimes dealerships), these "powder puff" courses are usually designed specifically for women.

# More Memory Tips

Someday, researchers suggest, it will be possible to go to your doctor and get a personally designed "exercise plan" for your brain to prevent your mental skills from deteriorating, much the way a physical therapist might devise a treatment plan to help a trick knee or bad back. Until then, gerontologists have a host of suggestions for things you can do to make life more stimulating and boost your memory.

If you want to memorize a speech or improve your memory for names, read the appropriate chapters in this book to learn specific techniques. They will work for young and old alike.

There are probably as many memory aids as there things to be remembered. As far back as the late 19th century, psychologist William James was busy coming up with ways to put some pizazz into his brain cells, and he came to the conclusion that it's possible to improve memory by improving the way facts are memorized . . . which is why every music teacher since has translated the notes on the lines of the musical scale (EGBDF) into "Every Good Boy Does Fine."

Here are some general tips from the experts to boost memory:

■ Don't cram. It's always better to sit down once or twice a day to try to remember things than to try to cram ten hours of study in at one time. No matter what method you use to remember the name of your new neighbor, your zip code, or the third law of quantum mechanics, the amount of time spent trying to remember is crucial.

■ Pay attention. People pay attention to what interests them. If you must read and remember something, try to find a room where you can read without too many distractions.

■ Be an *active* reader. If you want to remember written material, read each sentence as a critic would, ready to locate an inconsistency and checking the content against what you already know.

■ Keep a diary. If you have trouble remembering appointments, make sure every appointment is put into a calendar or diary—and be consistent. Keep the diary in the same place, and always enter every appointment. Make it a point to check the diary every day.

■ Try an alarm. If you have trouble remembering appointments, try setting a wristwatch alarm to go off shortly before each appointment.

■ Keep lists. Always keep a shopping list tacked on the wall, and always add items you need to the list. Keep lists of jobs, things to be done, etc.

■ Write notes. Write reminders to yourself and leave them in a prominent place.

■ Use your senses. If you really want to remember something, use as many senses as possible—smell, sound, sight, touch, and taste—to help impress upon yourself whatever you're trying to remember.

■ Relax. It's always more difficult to remember if you're in a tense, nervous state. Take a few deep breaths and consciously relax your muscles.

- Make conscious choices. Put extra energy and effort into remembering things that are important to you.

- Take your time. As we get older, it may take longer to remember something, but often the information will surface if you wait a moment and don't push yourself too hard. If you can't remember the details, admit you've forgotten—don't beat yourself up over it.

- Don't expect too much. If you're nervous about forgetting something, most likely you'll do just that.

- If you are worried about forgetting things, keep a diary to track the things you forget. This will probably show that your moments of forgetfulness are not nearly as frequent as they seemed, and it will pinpoint those areas in which you do tend to forget things.

# Remember to Take Medications

If you have trouble remembering to take your pills, it's very important to set up a system to take control of this problem. Medications taken incorrectly can have serious effects on your health.

The system you come up with will depend on the number of pills you must take and how often you must take them. You'll have to experiment to see what works for you. Some people cut up an old egg carton to create the correct number of compartments for the day's medications. It's also possible to purchase special pillboxes and compartmentalized containers that do the same job. But no matter what you use, it's important to:

- Label your container with the names of the pills you use.

- Place the container where you will see it right away.

- Put the required number of pills in the container each morning.

- Check the container at night to make sure all the pills have been taken.

- If you forget to take a pill, don't automatically take it with the next dose. Contact your pharmacist or physician to ask for directions.

- Take out enough pills for one day and keep the rest in the original container.

# What to Expect

If you were always a dunce when it came to mathematics, don't expect a few memory methods to turn you into Stephen Hawking. How much neurological bang you get for your buck depends on how much brainpower you have to start with and the reason why your memory has slowed down. If a memory problem is caused by any sort of brain disease, most memory strategies aren't going to help. But if the brain is structurally healthy, odds are these techniques will provide some improvement in memory and problem-solving skills.

A cautionary note: While there's no need for you to accept age-related mental decline as inevitable, be sensible. The lower energy level and stamina common in old age must be taken into consideration. "You have to set priorities," explains Dr. Schaie. "It's not possible to run, swim, and do brain exercises constantly. You have to make some choices."

Still, the outlook is far from bleak. By using the techniques in this book, older people can expect to regain what they feel they have lost. "Barring physical brain disease," Dr. Schaie says, "there's no reason for an older person to automatically lose control over [his or her] mental abilities."

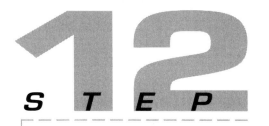

# Improve Your Memory Through Your Lifestyle

**M**ost people have problems with their memory on some days and not on others. When you're feeling alert, well rested and healthy, you're less likely to have problems in everyday remembering. But some days, when things haven't been going well and you're tense or depressed—maybe you have an ache or pain—you probably feel more off balance. Your mind might be preoccupied, or you might find yourself dwelling on negative thoughts or feelings. It's at these times that you're more likely to have problems in remembering.

While scientists still debate about the extent of interaction between mind and body, they are discovering more and more relationships between the way we feel and the way our bodies function.

Since memory is part of your cognitive process—how you think—it follows that anything that interferes with optimum brain function can also affect how well you store information in memory and how well you retrieve that information. You've already learned that the key to a good memory is to pay attention, so it stands to reason that any outside distraction or emotional concerns that interfere with attention will also interfere with how well you can remember.

It's also important to note that both your body and your mind—and hence your memory—are influenced by diet, medications, stress level, exercise, smoking, and relaxation.

# Stress and Memory

It's true that stress affects mood, and mood affects your ability to remember. Problems with remembering can produce even more stress, which further interferes with how well you can access your memory. In fact, anxiety and depression are the two major causes of memory problems at any age. This is because these psychological conditions take over, making it impossible to concentrate on anything else. When you're deeply depressed or overstressed, you tend to turn inward. You don't record information the way you normally would, and your thoughts are occupied with negative ruminations.

Anyone who has heard bad news in a doctor's office can attest to the fact that when stress and anxiety take over, it's very hard to remember anything.

When Sarah's surgeon revealed to her that she had breast cancer, she recalls that the next twenty minutes were a total blur to her. She heard virtually nothing that her doctor was telling her about her prognosis and treatment plan, because all she could think about was that she had cancer and was going to die.

Admittedly, the shock of a cancer diagnosis is great. But it is a good idea to try to tell yourself that you'll have to calm down and pay strict attention if you're going to remember what the doctor is saying.

# When Your Mind Goes Blank

Even fairly minor amounts of stress can interfere with memory. If you've got an important business appointment at nine in the morning and it will take you fifteen minutes to get there, you're bound to feel a buildup of stress when you can't remember where you left either your car keys or your briefcase. The more desperately you search, the more nervous and tense you become.

If you stand still and try to think where you left your keys, chances are you'll have a hard time remembering where they are, because the physical sensations of stress are interfering with your concentration. The harder you try to remember, the more likely you are to "go blank."

Susan was finishing an important proposal at work, but she was starting to have trouble finding just the right words. She was already feeling pressure about this project and she felt that each sentence had to be perfect. As the deadline approached, she began to have a harder and harder time finding the words she wanted. The more she struggled with that tip-of-the-tongue feeling, the more elusive those words became. As each moment passed, Sue's stress increased, which only blocked her remembering process even more.

If you're ever in this situation, you need to step back a moment from the stressful situation and consciously relax. This can be very difficult, especially if you're in the middle of a stress-filled day, but it's essential if you're going to get back on track.

## Practice Relaxation Techniques

First, practice slowing your breathing, so that you inhale deeply, slowly, and evenly. Breathing is especially important in achieving relaxation; it is almost impossible to feel stressed when you have successfully slowed down each breath.

Next, try "progressive relaxation." With this technique, you consciously relax each set of muscles, one at a time, beginning with the skin at the top of your head, then down around your face, your ears, and the back of your neck. Consciously lower and relax your shoulders, and then move down slowly, relaxing only one set of muscles at a time. By the time you reach your feet, you'll be surprised at how much calmer you feel. Many people are never truly aware how tense their muscles are until they consciously relax them.

Practice relaxation skills every day, so that when you need them they will be second nature. You can find courses in relaxation training at community centers, local colleges and universities, health centers, the YMCA or YWCA, etc. Swimming and walking are two other ways of helping yourself work off excess tension and stress.

# Diet and Memory

Ever since the Middle Ages, memory experts have believed that a good diet can enhance memory performance—although it was not always understood what a good "memory diet" really was. Nutritionists in the 15th century advised their clients to eat hearty food for a good memory—roasted fowl, apples, nuts, and red wine.

Today, scientists have a slightly different perspective on the role of nutrition and memory. It is certainly true that imbalances in diet can cause problems. A child's ability to remember can be affected by deficiencies in iron, minerals, vitamins, and protein,

## Visualization: The Key To Relaxation

Along with relaxation techniques, you may find that this visualization exercise can help you relax:

- Pick a comfortable chair and close your eyes.

- Imagine that you are at the beach. Visualize this scene using all of your senses.

- Listen to the roar of the ocean, the cry of the seagulls.

- Smell the salt air and feel the stinging sea spray on your face.

- Work your toes into the sand.

- Now begin to breathe deeply, bringing the fresh, clean sea air into your lungs. Breathe in time to the crashing of the waves on the shore, one after the other. Breathe out into the sea air.

- Listen closer to the sound of the waves, and the ebb and flow of the tide.

- Time your breathing to match the waves.

- Keep listening and breathing until you begin to feel relaxed.

and by food additives and too much sugar. In fact, deficiencies of almost any nutrient can impair the nervous system. Imbalances in certain vitamins and minerals also appear to play a part in memory problems.

# Drink Plenty of Water

But food is not the only important component of a good "memory diet." Water helps maintain memory systems, especially in older folks. Lack of water in the body has a direct and profound effect on memory; dehydration can lead to confusion and other thinking problems.

# Eat Right

While nutritionists today aren't sure exactly how diet affects memory, they do know that essential nutrients are important for enhancing chemical processes in the body, including registering, retaining, and remembering information. These essential nutrients include protein, carbohydrates, lecithin, and vitamin $B_1$.

But because scientists aren't sure if some of these foods are better at boosting memory than others, they advise that the best memory insurance is to eat a good, balanced diet—a variety of dairy products, bread and cereals, vegetable and fruit, and seafood, poultry, or meat. Without sufficient levels of thiamine, folic acid, and vitamin $B_{12}$, the brain can't function properly and experiences memory and concentration problems.

Some experts advocate using "memory nutrients" (choline, B-complex vitamins, iodine, manganese, and folic acid), although other researchers argue that studies have not yet proven that these nutrients work.

It is true that when foods rich in choline (liver, soybeans, lecithin, eggs, and fish) were fed to subjects in one study, their diet sparked an increase in acetylcholine, a brain chemical critical to the memory process. When these subjects took 10 grams of choline, they were able to recall a list of unrelated words more quickly than those who did not take choline. In other studies, patients with Alzheimer's disease showed improvements in memory when treated with choline.

There is some evidence from animal studies that low levels of vitamin $B_6$ and copper are related to deteriorating brain cells, which leads some researchers to conclude that mild deficiencies of these vitamins over the years might have the same effect in humans. And when researchers in New Mexico tested the memory ability of a group of normal elderly subjects, they found that those with the lowest levels of vitamins $B_{12}$ and C did poorly on memory tests. Those with the lowest levels of vitamins $B_{12}$ and C, riboflavin, and folate scored the worst on problem-solving tests.

Zinc, as well, appears to be related to memory. In studies of 1,200 patients over age fifty, the 220 senile people in the group had significantly lower zinc levels than those who weren't senile.

## Don't Overeat

It's not a good idea to eat large amounts of food right before beginning a thinking task. Loading up the stomach impairs performance and distracts the mind during the critical registration and remembering phases. Experts advise eating only a light meal before giving a speech, taking a test, or attending a class.

# Sleep and Memory

While the tendency is to stay up late at night and cram for a test or a business presentation the next day, in fact the best thing you can do to ensure a good memory is get plenty of rest. While you're asleep, your memory is being revised and stored in the brain. This is why you may find that you suddenly wake up with an answer to a problem that has been worrying you during the day—your brain doesn't sleep at night while the rest of you does.

In order to function with peak memory skills, it is essential to get enough sleep and rest the brain. During certain periods of deep sleep that occur about every hour and a half, the brain disconnects from the senses and processes, reviews, consolidates, and stores memory. To interfere with this crucial time of sleep will seriously affect subsequent performance.

Insomnia (the inability to sleep) not only deprives a person of the valuable memory consolidation periods during rest; it also interferes with learning during waking hours as well. This problem affects the elderly in particular, who often have many sleep problems and get very little deep sleep—the period of time when the brain recharges itself. After a while, a person who doesn't get good sleep begins to live in a chronic state of fatigue and finds it difficult to pay attention or register information.

# Medication and Memory

There are some drugs that can affect memory (especially when taken by older people)—particularly the benzodiazepines, which include diazepam (Valium) and lorazepam (Ativan). Benzodiazepines promote sleep and reduce anxiety, but they can impair memory and other aspects of mental function. For example, when Ativan is taken at night to fall asleep, patients experience a small memory impairment the next morning.

Under certain circumstances, the benzodiazepines can induce a temporary amnesic state that interferes with learning shortly after taking the drug. Of course, the ability of these drugs to induce this sort of amnesia can be used to the patient's advantage in a medical setting. Some dentists, for example, use intravenous Valium for patients who fear dental surgery. Not only does the drug reduce anxiety, but patients have trouble recalling the surgery itself, which is helpful if they need to face further surgery.

While drugs are designed to treat medical problems, most have some side effects. Two or more drugs taken together can interact with each other, and the resulting reaction can be unpredictable. Some of these side effects, especially in older people, can have a significant impact on memory and other intellectual functioning.

Muscle relaxants, tranquilizers, sleeping pills, and anti-anxiety drugs may sometimes produce confusion and memory loss. As a general rule, any medication that warns you not to drive when taking the drug may impair your ability to remember. Even non-prescription medications (like cold tablets or allergy pills) that contain antihistamines can induce drowsiness and affect the ability to remember.

Some cardiac drugs (such as propranolol, which is used to control high blood pressure) can cause depression and memory problems.

And sometimes during anesthesia, if the patient does not get enough oxygen, temporary memory problems can occur in the days following the anesthesia. This is because it may take several days for the anesthetics to be eliminated from the system.

If you are having memory problems and you are taking medications, check with your doctor or pharmacist to see if the medications may be contributing to the problem.

### How to Avoid Medication-Related Memory Problems

- Fill all prescriptions at the same pharmacy. This will help your pharmacist recognize potentially problematic drug interactions.

- Bring a list of all your drugs to your doctor's office. Include *all* nonprescription drugs, vitamins, and supplements that you take.

- Follow your doctor's prescription. If you miss a dose, never double the next one without your doctor's approval.

- Don't combine alcohol and medications—not even over-the-counter pills—but especially not drugs that affect the central nervous system (tranquilizers, sedatives, barbiturates, etc.).

- Avoid chronic use of laxatives; this can lead to a chemical imbalance that may cause confusion, affecting memory.

# Alcohol and Memory

Studies have shown that even a few drinks four times a week will interfere with the ability to remember. Unfortunately, the problem is much more serious for the nation's alcoholics. Alcoholism is one of the most serious and prevalent medical problems in the United States, and it causes serious memory problems. Statistics suggest that at least 12 to 15 percent of the population may be alcoholics.

Short-term memory loss is a classic problem among those who abuse alcohol, which impairs the ability to retain new information. This potential deficit is based not on the number of ounces drunk each day, but on your own specific tolerance for alcohol. And as you get older, the effects of drinking may change despite the fact that you aren't drinking any more than you ever have. Among older people, the amount of alcohol in the body builds up more quickly, and the effects remain longer.

In studies at the University of California at Los Angeles, scientists discovered that people over age forty experience the most memory problems after drinking—but even people between the ages of twenty-one and thirty experience some memory loss. In addition, women appear to be more susceptible to the toxic effects of alcohol, especially in relation to short-term memory performance.

Most alcohol-induced memory problems seem to disappear when the person stops drinking, although a lifetime of abuse may cause irreversible damage.

Chronic alcohol abuse may lead to a condition called Wernicke's encephalopathy, which is characterized by sudden onset of confusion, memory problems, and loss of sensation that, if untreated, may be fatal. If treatment is not begun soon enough, the patient may develop Korsakoff's psychosis (or syndrome), with severe amnesia and disorientation. Recent memories are affected more than distant ones, and patients often can't remember what they did even a few moments ago.

# Smoking and Memory

It's a fact that smoking cuts down on the amount of oxygen that reaches the brain. In this way, it can interfere with memory. Studies have shown that smokers consistently score lower on memory tests than nonsmokers, and tests of name and face recall reveal that both visual and verbal memory is impaired in those who smoke more than a pack of cigarettes a day.

# Caffeine and Memory

While the amount of caffeine in coffee or tea is a mild stimulant and may keep you awake enough to pay attention, it's just as likely to have a negative impact on memory, because it provokes agitation that interferes with memory function. Studies have shown that a person who is already wide awake and rested won't get much of a memory boost from caffeine. But too much coffee (the exact amount differs from one person to the next) can cause significant memory problems. For a habitual user, however, abstaining may have the same negative effect.

In fact, a study of college students showed that drinking caffeine lowered their ability to remember a list of words.

Caffeine acts on the brain in ways that affect coordination, concentration, sleep patterns, and behavior. The gastrointestinal tract absorbs almost all caffeine and distributes it to all tissues and organs within minutes of drinking or eating the substance. Caffeine peaks in the blood within forty-five minutes, but its effects depend on the amount consumed, how often it is consumed, how much the body absorbs, and how quickly it is metabolized.

No matter what it may do to your memory, however, it's hard to avoid. Caffeine is present in a huge number of products—everything from painkillers to chocolate bars. It is found in more than 2,000 over-the-counter drugs and 1,000 prescription drugs.

It may not be easy at first, but moderating your lifestyle—eating right, drinking fluids, getting rest and relaxation, avoiding harmful substances—can really have an impact on you *and* your memory.

# Glossary

**abstract memory**  A person's general store of knowledge. This type of memory has a huge capacity for storing meanings of events and objects. Damage to certain parts of your brain (including certain parts of the cortex) can affect abstract memory.

**acalculia**  A specific impairment in dealing with arithmetical concepts.

**acetylcholine**  A type of brain chemical (or neurotransmitter) that may play a role in learning and memory by helping brain cells in the cortex retain the imprint of incoming information. Acetylcholine is vital for the transmission of messages from one nerve cell to another.

**acquisition**  The process of encoding or recording information, which is the first step in the memory process. It is followed by storage and retrieval (or recall). People who have problems remembering may have a problem with acquisition if the information was never recorded in the first place; memory loss, however, is usually caused by a problem in retrieval.

**agnosia**  A neurological problem in which patients fail to recognize objects even though they show no sign of sensory impairment. There are different types of agnosia—for example, facial agnosia or prosopagnosia (in which patients can't recognize a familiar face but can recognize the person's voice).

**agraphia**   The loss or reduction in the ability to write, despite normal hand and arm muscle function. It is caused by brain damage to the part of the brain that handles writing.

**alexia**   The inability to recognize and name written words by a person who had been literate. This disorder severely interferes with the ability to read. It is caused by stroke or head injury to a part of the cerebrum.

▪ **alphabetical searching**   A type of verbal memory method in which a person works through the alphabet in hopes that a particular letter will act as a retrieval cue for a forgotten word or name. It is effective only when a person has a great deal of information about the word (length, commonness, number of syllables, etc.).

**apraxia**   Loss of previous ability to perform skilled motor acts not explained by weakness or abnormal muscles. It is caused by nerve damage within the main mass of the brain in areas responsible for translating the idea of a movement into that movement.

**episodic memory**   Memories of personal events, such as a first dance or where one learned to ride a bike.

▪ **first-letter cueing**   The use of the first letter of a word as a cue to remember the word itself. This technique usually employs acronyms or acrostics.

**flashbulb memory**   A memory formed in relation to dramatic or emotionally upsetting events. The memory is sharply etched in the mind because it involves a sudden powerful emotion— shock, anger, disbelief, outrage. Scientists believe that these memories are encoded differently from everyday memories. The more muted the emotion, the less powerful and enduring the memory.

▪ **link system**   The most basic of all memory systems, used for memorizing short lists of items, such as shopping lists. Each item is linked to, or associated with, the next.

✦ **loci, method of**   The oldest memory system known, in which items to be remembered are mentally placed in an imaginary space. To recall the item, the person simply recalls the location. The method of loci was the most popular system until about the middle of the 1600s.

**long-term memory**   A type of memory consisting of many layers of memories that last indefinitely. Scientists believe that what a person chooses to store in long-term memory is probably closely tied to the emotions.

**mnemonic**   Any system or technique that aids the memory.

✦ **peg word system**   A type of visual imagery technique for improving learning in which a standard set of peg words are learned. Items to be remembered are linked to the pegs with visual imagery.

**phonetic system**   A mnemonic system that relies on the relationship between numbers and their consonant sounds.

**photographic memory**   The long-term persistence of mental imagery. Also known as eidetic memory.

**procedural memory**   The ability to remember how to do something, such as ride a bike or write a letter.

**semantic memory**   Mental storage of factual information, such as the capital of Pennsylvania or the multiplication tables, without connection to where or when one learned the information.

**short-term memory**   Another word for consciousness; also referred to as immediate or working memory. If not processed further, information in short-term memory quickly fades away.

✦ **verbal elaboration**   Comments, analysis, judgments, and so on that enhance the recording of a memory trace. Verbal elaboration gets a person involved emotionally and intellectually, ensuring a vibrant memory trace.

**verbal memory strategies**   Internal methods for remembering. Some of the best known are alphabetical searching and first-letter cueing, which are often helpful in coming up with something in the wake of the tip-of-the-tongue phenomenon.

**visual alphabet**   A way of representing letters of the alphabet by images formed in various ways, such as a picture of an object whose shape resembles a letter of the alphabet.

**visual association**   A memory strategy used to help make image associations in order to improve recall for many different types of information. By associating images with many contexts, it is possible to improve recall. Visual imagery by itself is not very effective; visual associations are most effective if they interact and are vivid.

**visual memory**   A very vivid type of memory for images that capture a person's attention. Most people almost never forget a face, even if they see it only once.

**visual peg system**   A type of visual imagery method that has been used since ancient times, in which numbers are associated with an unchanging set of words, or pegs. The items to be re- membered are then linked to these pegs.

# Bibliography

Adelson, B. "When novices surpass experts: The difficulty of a task may increase with expertise." Journal of Experimental Psychology: Learning, Memory, and Cognition 9 (1983): 422–33.

Adler, Tina. "Additional information can distort memories." APA Monitor (October 1989), 12–13.

———. "Memory software explains failings." APA Monitor (December 1989) 6.

———. "Implicit memory seems to age well." APA Monitor (February 1990) 8.

———. "Ability to store memory linked to glucose levels." APA Monitor (September 1990) 5–6.

———. "Psychologists examine aging, cognitive change." APA Monitor (November 1990) 4–5.

Albert, M. S., and M. Moss. "The assessment of memory disorders in patients with Alzheimer's disease." In Neuropsychology of Memory, edited by L. R. Squire and N. Butters, 236–46. New York: Guilford, 1984.

Alkon, Daniel L. "Memory storage and neural systems: Electrical and chemical changes which accompany conditioning applied to artificial network designs." Scientific American (July 1989), 42–51.

Allport, Susan. Explorers of the Black Box: The Search for the Cellular Basis of Memory. New York: W. W. Norton and Co., 1986.

American Management Association. How to Build Memory Skills. New York: Education for Management, 1978.

Anderson, J. R. Cognitive Psychology and Its Implications. New York: Freeman Press, 1985.

Anderson, J. R., and G. H. Bower. Human Associative Memory. Washington: Winston, 1972.

Arnold, M. B. Memory and the Brain. Hillsdale, N.J.: Lawrence Erlbaum Associates, 1984.

Aronson, Ed. D. Understanding Alzheimer's Disease. New York: Scribner's, 1988.

Baddeley, Alan. The Psychology of Memory. New York: Basic Books, 1976.

————. Your Memory—A User's Guide. New York: Macmillan Publishing Co., 1982; Emmaus, PA: Rodale Press, 1991.

————. "The psychology of remembering and forgetting." In Memory. Oxford: Basil Blackwell, 1989.

————. "Working memory." Science 255 (January 31, 1992): 556–59.

Bagne, C. A., N. Pomara, T. Crook, and S. Gershon. Treatment Development Strategies of Alzheimer's Disease. New Canaan, Conn.: Mark Powley Associates, 1986.

Barron, Susan. "Fear of forgetting: Why you lose your memory and some solutions." Washingtonian (May 1989), 150–58.

Bartlett, F. C. Remembering. Cambridge: Cambridge University Press, 1932.

Bartus, R. T., R. L. Dean, K. A. Sherman, E. Friedman, and B. Beer. "Profound effects of combining choline and piracetam on memory enhancement and cholinergic function in aged rats." Neurobiology of Aging 2 (1981): 105–11.

Bartus, R. T., R. L. Dean, B. Beer, and A. S. Lippa. "The cholinergic hypothesis of geriatric memory dysfunction." Science 217 (1982): 408.

Begley, Sharon, John Carey, and Ray Sawhill. "How the brain works." Newsweek (February 7, 1983), 40–47.

Begley, Sharon,. "Thinking looks like this." Newsweek (November 25, 1991), 67.

Bellezza, F. S. Improve Your Memory Skills. Englewood Cliffs, N.J.: Prentice Hall, 1982.

Birren, J. E., and K. W. Schaie. Handbook of the Psychology of Aging. New York: Van Nostrand Reinhold, 1977.

Blakeslee, Sandra. "Memories are made of this." New Choices for the Best Years (November 1989), 41–45.

Blumenthal, J. A., and D. J. Madden. "Effects of aerobic exercise training, age, and physical fitness on memory-search performance." Psychology and Aging 3 (1988): 280–85.

Bolles, Edmund Blair. Remembering and Forgetting: Inquiries into the Nature of Memory. New York: Walker and Co., 1988.

———. So Much to Say. New York: St. Martin's Press, 1982.

Botwinick, Jack, and Martha Storandt. Memory, Related Functions, and Age. Springfield, Ill.: Charles C. Thomas Publisher, 1974.

Bower, Bruce. "Boosting memory in the blink of an eye." Science News 135 (February 11, 1989): 86.

———. "Weak memories make strong comeback." Science News 138 (July 21, 1990): 36.

———. "Gone but not forgotten: Scientists uncover pervasive, unconscious influences on memory." Science News 138 (November 17, 1990): 312–15.

———. "Focused attention boosts depressed memory." Science News 140 (September 7, 1991): 151.

———. "Monitoring memories moving in the brain." Science News 141 (May 2, 1992): 294.

Brayne, C., and D. Calloway. "Normal aging, impaired cognitive function and senile dementia of the Alzheimer's type: A continuum?" Lancet 1 (1988): 1265–66.

Brewer, W. F., and J. C. Treyens. "Role of schemata in memory for places." Cognitive Psychology 13 (1981): 207–30.

Burg, Bob. "Six steps to remembering what's-his-name." ABA Banking Journal (September 1990), 92.

————. The Memory System: Remember Everything You Need When You Need It. Shawnee Mission, Kans.: National Seminars Publications, 1992.

Buzan, Tony. Use Your Perfect Memory. New York: E. P. Dutton, 1984.

Bylinsky, G. "Medicine's next marvel: The memory pill." Fortune, (January 20, 1986), 68–72.

Cassedy, Ellen. "It isn't lost; I just can't find it." Woman's Day (October 2, 1990), 40–43.

Cermak, Laird S. Improving Your Memory. New York: W. W. Norton and Co., 1975.

————. Human Memory and Amnesia. Hillsdale, N.J.: Erlbaum, 1982.

Christensen, H., and A. Mackinnon. "The association between mental, social, and physical activity and cognitive performance in young and old subjects." Age and Aging 22 (May 1993): 175–82.

Clark, Linda. Help Yourself to Health. New York: Pyramid Books, 1976.

Cohen, Gillian. Memory in the Real World. London: Lawrence Erlbaum Associates, 1989.

DeAngelis, Tori. "Dietary recall is poor, survey study suggests." APA Monitor (December 1988), 14.

Denton, Laurie. "Mood's role in memory still puzzling." APA Monitor (November 1987), 18.

Diagram Group. The Brain: A User's Manual. New York: G. P. Putnam and Sons, 1982.

Edson, Lee. How We Learn. New York: Time-Life Books, 1975.

Erikson, G. C., et al. "The effects of caffeine on memory for word lists." Physiology and Behavior 35 (1985): 47–51.

Fisher, Kathy. "Learning and memory: brain structure." APA Monitor (September 1990), 3, 6, 7.

Furst, Bruno. Stop Forgetting. Garden City: Doubleday and Co., 1979.

Gallant, Roy A. Memory: How It Works and How to Improve It. New York: Four Winds Press, 1980.

Gose, Kathleen, and Gloria Levi. Dealing with Memory Changes As You Grow Older. New York: Bantam Books, 1988.

Hales, Dianne. "Why don't I remember?" McCall's (February 1990), 75–77.

Herrmann, Douglas J. Super Memory: A Quick-Action Program for Memory Improvement. Emmaus, Pa.: Rodale Press, 1991.

Heston, Leonard L., and June A. White. Dementia: A Practical Guide to Alzheimer's Disease and Related Illnesses. New York: W. H. Freeman and Co., 1983.

Higbee, Kenneth L. Your Memory: How It Works and How to Improve It. New York: Simon and Schuster, 1988.

———. Your Memory. New York: Prentice Hall, 1988.

Hines, William. "Brain tumors and their many different paths." The Washington Post Health Magazine (April 7, 1987), 8–9.

Hostetler, A. J. "Try to remember . . . a computer battery is helping test drugs' effects on Alzheimer's." APA Monitor (May 1987), 18.

———. "Exploring the 'gatekeeper' of memory: Changes in hippocampus seen in aging, amnesia, Alzheimer's." APA Monitor (April 1988), 3.

Job, Eena. Fending Off Forgetfulness: A Practical Guide to Improving Memory. London: University of Queensland Press, 1985.

Klatzky, Robert L. Human Memory: Structures and Processes. New York: W. H. Freeman, 1980.

Krassner, Michael B. "Diet and brain function." Nutrition Reviews, supplement (May 1986): 12–15.

Krauthammer, Charles. "Disorders of memory." Time (July 3, 1989), 74.

Landers, Susan. "Memories of elderly found to be accurate in surveys." APA Monitor (October 1987), 15.

Lapp, Danielle. (Nearly) Total Recall: A Guide to a Better Memory at Any Age. Stanford: Stanford Alumni Association, 1992.

Loftus, Elizabeth. Memory: Surprising New Insights into How We Remember and Why We Forget. Reading, Mass.: Addison-Wesley Publishing Co., 1980.

————. Memory. Reading, Mass.: Addison-Wesley Publishing Co, 1980.

Loftus, E. F., and E. Greene. "Warning: Even memory for faces may be contagious." Law and Human Behavior 4 (1980): 323–34.

Loftus, E. F., and G. R. Loftus. "On the permanence of stored information in the human brain." American Psychologist 35 (1980): 421–34.

Loftus, E. F., and W. Marburger. "Since the eruption of Mount St. Helens has anyone beaten you up? Improving the accuracy of retrospective reports with landmark events." Memory and Cognition 2 (1983), 114–20.

Lorayne, Harry, and Jerry Lucas. The Memory Book. New York: Dorset Press, 1974.

Lorayne, Harry. Remembering People. New York: Stein and Day, 1975.

Mace, Nancy, and Peter Rabins. The 36-Hour Day: A Guide to Caring for Persons with Alzheimer's Disease and Related Dementing Illnesses. Baltimore: Johns Hopkins University Press, 1991.

Mantyla, T. "Knowing but not remembering: Adult age differences in recollective expression." Memory and Cognition 21 (May 1993): 379–88.

Mark, Vernon, and Jeffrey P. Mark. "Why we forget: Ten common and reversible causes of memory loss." Modern Maturity (August-September 1990), 70–74.

Markowitsch, H. J. "Hypotheses on mnemonic information processing by the brain." International Journal of Neuroscience 15 (1985): 189–287.

Mayes, Andrew R. Human Organic Memory Disorders, Cambridge: Cambridge University Press, 1988.

Minninger, Joan. Total Recall: How to Boost Your Memory Power. Emmaus, Pa.: Rodale Press, 1984.

Noll, Richard, and Carol Turkington. The Encyclopedia of Memory and Memory Disorders. New York: Facts on File, 1994.

Ostrander, Sheila, and Lynn Schroeder. Super-Memory: The Revolution. New York: Carroll and Graf Publishers, 1991.

Parkin, Alan J. Memory and Amnesia. Oxford: Basil Blackwell, 1987.

Pelton, R., and T. C. Pelton. Mind Food and Smart Pills. New York: Doubleday, 1989.

Pool, J. L. Nature's Masterpiece: The Brain and How It Works. New York: Walker and Company, 1987.

Poole, Robert, ed. The Incredible Machine. Washington: National Geographic Society, 1986.

Restak, Richard. The Brain. New York: Bantam Books, 1984.

Richardson, John T. E. Mental Imagery and Human Memory. New York: St. Martin's Press, 1980.

Richman, Barbara. "Memorable mnemonic." APA Monitor (October 1986), 16.

Rosenfield, Israel. The Invention of Memory: A New View of the Brain. New York: Basic Books, 1989.

Saline, Carol. "Remembrance of things, uh . . . uh . . . well, hmm . . ." Philadelphia Magazine (May 1992), 49–53.

Sangiorgio, Maureen, Greg Gutfeld, and Linda Rao. "Aerobic memory: Exercises and memory." Prevention (February 1992), 14–15.

Schooler, J., and E. Loftus. "Memory." In McGraw-Hill Encyclopedia of Science and Technology, Vol. 10. New York: McGraw-Hill Book Co., 1987.

Simons, Marlise. "Le brain jogging." New York Times Magazine (October 6, 1991), 44.

Smith, Charles. "Your memory: Don't leave home without it." American Salesman (October 1990), 3–5.

Squire, L. R., and N. J. Cohen. "Remote memory, retrograde amnesia and the neuropsychology of memory." In Human Memory and Amnesia. Hillsdale, N.J.: Erlbaum, 1982.

Squire, Larry R., and N. Butters. Neuropsychology of Memory. New York: Guilford Press, 1984.

Watson, Ronald R. "Caffeine: Is it dangerous to health?" American Journal of Health Promotion 2 (Spring 1988): 13–21.

Weintraub, Pamela. "Total recall: Ways to improve your memory." American Health (March 1992), 77–83.

Weiss, Robert J., and Genell Subak-Sharpe. The Complete Guide to Health and Well-being After 50. New York: G. S. Sharpe Communications, 1988.

"When to worry about forgetting." Harvard Health Letter (July 1992), 1–3.

Wilson, B., and N. Moffat. Clinical Management of Memory Problems. Rockville, Md.: Aspen Systems, 1984.

Wilson, B. The Rehabilitation of Memory. New York: Guilford Press, 1987.

Yates, Frances A. The Art of Memory. Chicago: University of Chicago Press, 1966.